The Sermon on the Mount

The Sermon on the Mount

Matthew 5–7

Clifford M. Yeary
with Little Rock Scripture Study staff

LITURGICAL PRESS
Collegeville, Minnesota

www.littlerockscripture.org

Nihil obstat: Reverend Robert Harren, J.C.L., *Censor deputatus.*
Imprimatur: ✛ Most Reverend Donald J. Kettler, J.C.L., Bishop of Saint Cloud, August 14, 2019.

Cover design by John Vineyard. Interior art by Ned Bustard.

 This symbol indicates material that was created by Little Rock Scripture Study to supplement the biblical text and commentary. Some of these inserts first appeared in the *Little Rock Catholic Study Bible*; others were created specifically for this book by Amy Ekeh and Catherine Upchurch.

1	2	3	4	5	6	7	8	9

Library of Congress Cataloging-in-Publication Data

Names: Yeary, Clifford M., author. | Little Rock Scripture Study Staff, author.
Title: The sermon on the mount : Matthew 5-7 / Clifford M. Yeary with Little Rock Scripture Study staff.
Description: Collegeville : Liturgical Press, 2020. | Includes bibliographical references. | Summary:
  "Profound discipleship is not just for those destined for canonization. The Sermon on the Mount
  challenges us to hear Jesus speaking to us, calling us to constant conversion and urging us to transform
  our world"—Provided by publisher.
Identifiers: LCCN 2019029938 (print) | LCCN 2019029939 (ebook) | ISBN 9780814644003 (paperback) |
  ISBN 9780814644997 (ebook)
Subjects: LCSH: Sermon on the mount--Study and teaching.
Classification: LCC BT380.3 .Y4335 2020 (print) | LCC BT380.3 (ebook) | DDC 226.9/06—dc23
LC record available at https://lccn.loc.gov/2019029938
LC ebook record available at https://lccn.loc.gov/2019029939

TABLE OF CONTENTS

 Wrap-Up Lectures and Discussion Tips for Facilitators are available for each lesson at no charge. Find them online at LittleRockScripture.org/Lectures/SermonontheMount.

Welcome

The Bible is at the heart of what it means to be a Christian. It is the Spirit-inspired word of God for us. It reveals to us the God who created, redeemed, and guides us still. It speaks to us personally and as a church. It forms the basis of our public liturgical life and our private prayer lives. It urges us to live worthily and justly, to love tenderly and wholeheartedly, and to be a part of building God's kingdom here on earth.

Though it was written a long time ago, in the context of a very different culture, the Bible is no relic of the past. Catholic biblical scholarship is among the best in the world, and in our time and place, we have unprecedented access to it. By making use of solid scholarship, we can discover much about the ancient culture and religious practices that shaped those who wrote the various books of the Bible. With these insights, and by praying with the words of Scripture, we allow the words and images to shape us as disciples. By sharing our journey of faithful listening to God's word with others, we have the opportunity to be stretched in our understanding and to form communities of love and learning. Ultimately, studying and praying with God's word deepens our relationship with Christ.

The Sermon on the Mount
Matthew 5–7

The resource you hold in your hands is divided into four lessons. Each lesson involves personal prayer and study using this book *and* the experience of group prayer, discussion, and wrap-up lecture.

If you are using this resource in the context of a small group, we suggest that you meet four times, discussing one lesson per meeting. Allow about 90 minutes for the small group gathering. Small groups function best with eight to twelve people to ensure good group dynamics and to allow all to participate as they wish.

Some groups choose to have an initial gathering before their regular sessions begin. This allows an opportunity to meet one another, pass out books, and, if desired, view the optional intro lecture for this study available on the "Resources" page of the Little Rock Scripture Study website (www.littlerockscripture.org).

WHAT MATERIALS WILL YOU USE?

The materials in this book include:

- The text of Matthew 5–7, using the New American Bible, Revised Edition as the translation.

- Commentary by Clifford M. Yeary.

- Occasional inserts ⚫ highlighting elements of the chapters of Matthew being studied. Some of these appear also in the *Little Rock Catholic Study Bible* while others are supplied by staff writers.

- Questions for study, reflection, and discussion at the end of each lesson.

- Opening and closing prayers for each lesson, as well as other prayer forms available in the closing pages of the book.

In addition, there are wrap-up lectures available for each lesson. Your group may choose to purchase a DVD containing these lectures or make use of the audio or video lectures online at no charge. The link to these free lectures is: LittleRockScripture.org/Lectures/SermonontheMount. Of course, if your group has access to qualified speakers, you may choose to have live presentations.

Each person will need a current translation of the Bible. We recommend the *Little Rock Catholic Study Bible*, which makes use of the New American Bible, Revised Edition. Other translations, such as the New Jerusalem Bible or the New Revised Standard Version: Catholic Edition, would also work well.

HOW WILL YOU USE THESE MATERIALS?

Prepare in advance

Using Lesson One as an example:

- Begin with a simple prayer like the one found on page 11.

- Read the assigned material in the printed book for Lesson One (pages 12–24) so that you are prepared for the weekly small group session. You may do this assignment by reading a portion over a period of several days (effective and manageable) or by preparing all at once (more challenging).

- Answer the questions, Exploring Lesson One, found at the end of the assigned reading, pages 25–27.

- Use the Closing Prayer on page 27 when you complete your study. This prayer may be used again when you meet with the group.

Meet with your small group

- After introductions and greetings, allow time for prayer (about 5 minutes) as you begin the group session. You may use the prayer found on page 11 (also used by individuals in their preparation) or use a prayer of your choosing.

- Spend about 45–50 minutes discussing the responses to the questions that were prepared in advance. You may also develop your discussion further by responding to questions and interests that arise during the discussion and faith-sharing itself.

- Close the discussion and faith-sharing with prayer, about 5–10 minutes. You may use the Closing Prayer at the end of each lesson or one of your choosing at the end of the book. It is important to allow people to pray for personal and community needs and to give thanks for how God is moving in your lives.

- Listen to or view the wrap-up lecture associated with each lesson (15–20 minutes). You may watch the lecture online, use a DVD, or provide a live lecture by a qualified local speaker. This lecture provides a common focus for the group and reinforces insights from each lesson. You may view the lecture together at the end of the session or, if your group runs out of time, you may invite group members to watch the lecture on their own time after the discussion.

Above all, be aware that the Holy Spirit is moving within and among you.

The Sermon on the Mount

LESSON ONE

Introduction and Matthew 5:1-12

Begin your personal study and group discussion with a simple and sincere prayer such as:

Prayer

Jesus, you teach us to listen to your words and imitate your deeds. Be with me now as I listen for your voice, and help me to become more like you.

Read the Introduction on page 12 and the Bible text of Matthew 5:1-12 found in the outside columns of pages 13–23, highlighting what stands out to you.

Read the accompanying commentary to add to your understanding.

Respond to the questions on pages 25–27, Exploring Lesson One.

The Closing Prayer on page 27 is for your personal use and may be used at the end of group discussion.

INTRODUCTION

After hearing the Sermon on the Mount, "the crowds were astonished at his teaching, for he taught them as one having authority" (Matt 7:28b-29a). Christians today sometimes undermine the authority of Jesus by setting aside the necessity of living many of the Beatitudes and moral teachings expressed in the Sermon on the Mount. For centuries, many Christians have been taught that what Jesus proclaimed in the Sermon on the Mount were "evangelical virtues," ideals for those rare disciples who dared to live beyond the minimum that a just God required of the vast majority of his children.

For example, when Jesus said to "be perfect, just as your heavenly Father is perfect" (5:48), was he just giving encouragement to his most dedicated disciples, or was he telling all who would ever claim to be among his followers what was required of them? Understanding what Jesus meant by "be perfect" may help us understand his expectations. The root of the Greek word that is often translated into English as "perfect" suggests the kind of perfection that grows out of maturity or develops into wholeness. While none of us will ever be perfect in the way we typically think of perfection, especially in comparison to God's own perfection, we can all strive to mature as disciples.

Matthew opens the Sermon on the Mount by distinguishing between two audiences that gathered at the feet of Jesus to hear his teachings: there were disciples and there was also a crowd. The disciples were the ones Jesus had personally chosen, such as Peter and Andrew, James and John, as well as others who had committed to following Jesus. The crowds had either witnessed or heard of his miraculous powers and were coming to him for a variety of reasons. Many may simply have hoped to be amazed. In Matthew and elsewhere in the gospels, the crowds are quick to be amazed and even to hail Jesus as the Son of David, but they are just as quick to shout, "Let him be crucified!" (27:22-23).

In distinguishing between the two audiences, Matthew may well have desired to provoke a question in the minds of those early Christians for whom he wrote his gospel: am I listening to Jesus' words as a disciple or as someone in the crowd? Those of us who identify ourselves as Christians have no option but to listen and respond to Jesus' teachings as disciples. But we are disciples who must grow into our calling.

Jesus recognizes that his disciples have a lot of maturing to do. He chides them for the smallness of their faith five times in Matthew, including once within the Sermon on the Mount:

> "Why are you anxious about clothes? Learn from the way the wild flowers grow. They do not work or spin. But I tell you that not even Solomon in all his splendor was clothed like one of them. If God so clothes the grass of the field, which grows today and is thrown into the oven tomorrow, will he not much more provide for you, *O you of little faith*?" (6:28-30, emphasis mine)

In calling us to perfection, Jesus calls us to grow and mature. He knew that even his disciples would fail him, but, being perfect like his Father, Jesus never gave up on his disciples. That is why we have the Sermon on the Mount: to encourage us to grow into our calling, a calling to perfection that came to each of us in our baptism. I invite you to ponder the Sermon on the Mount with a sincere desire to be transformed by it. Perfection may be a long way off for many of us, especially me, but in writing this commentary I discovered the joy of believing the assurance Paul made to the Philippians: "I am confident of this, that the one who began a good work in you will continue to complete it until the day of Christ Jesus" (1:6).

5:1-12 THE BEATITUDES

Matthew introduces the Sermon on the Mount in the brevity of two sentences. In the first sentence we learn that there are two distinct groups to whom Jesus addresses his sermon: "When he saw the crowds, he went up the mountain, and after he had sat down, his disciples came to him" (5:1).

Immediately preceding the Sermon on the Mount, Matthew had just begun to tell of Jesus' ministry following his baptism and temptation. Having called his first disciples, Jesus preached the good news of the kingdom in synagogues around Galilee and cured everyone brought to him, regardless of what ailed them (4:23-24). Not surprisingly, this attracted a great deal of attention, and soon crowds gathered around him wherever he appeared. Matthew does not tell us exactly where the Sermon on the Mount occurred, choosing instead simply to affirm that "he went up the mountain" to deliver it after taking note of the crowd that has followed him. But the crowds are not the primary audience of his sermon. The Beatitudes and all the other teachings that follow in this sermon are primarily intended as instructions to his disciples, who "came to [Jesus]" before he began preaching (5:1-2).

The response to the Sermon on the Mount has remained the same throughout time. We

---

CHAPTER 5

The Sermon on the Mount

¹When he saw the crowds, he went up the mountain, and after he had sat down, his disciples came to him. ²He began to teach them, saying:

continue

---

are as astonished today as those who first heard it: "When Jesus finished these words, the crowds were astonished at his teaching, for he taught them as one having authority, and not as their scribes" (7:28-29).

The authority with which Jesus teaches is stunning. This authority is first hinted at by the fact that Jesus delivers his teaching on a mountain and in a seated position. The many Jewish Christians who would have first heard Matthew's recounting of the sermon would be quick to think of Moses. The great prophet and teacher of Israel was tasked on "the mountain" (Exod 3:1-2) with revealing God to the people of God, and later, "the LORD summoned Moses to the top of the mountain," where he received the law (Exod 19:20). Centuries later, Jesus, having gone up another mountain, sits down. This was the proper posture of a religious teacher. By Jesus' time, religious authorities in Israel were said to teach from the chair of Moses (Matt 23:2). To this day, universities endow their most honored professors with a "chair."

We are therefore alerted to just how authoritative Jesus' instruction will be: no one since Moses has ever taught like this before. As the impact of Jesus' teaching reaches us, we will discover that he interprets crucial aspects of the Mosaic covenant in a way that summons the prophetic words of Jeremiah:

See, days are coming—oracle of the LORD— when I will make a new covenant with the house of Israel and the house of Judah. It will not be like the covenant I made with their ancestors the day I took them by the hand to lead them out of the land of Egypt. They broke my covenant, though I was their master—oracle of the LORD. But this is the covenant I will make with the house of Israel after those days—oracle of the LORD. I will place my law within them, and write it upon their hearts; I will be their God, and they shall be my people. (Jer 31:31-33)

Matthew's introduction to the Beatitudes actually comes with a warning: we can position ourselves to listen to Jesus in one of two ways—the way of the crowd or the way of the disciples. The crowd hears Jesus and is amazed at his authority and the loftiness of the ideals his words express (7:28-29), but hearing his words does not make them disciples (7:21). Jesus expects those who follow him to accept his teachings as commandments, and his commandments go far beyond what the law of Moses demanded.

Each beatitude begins with the words "Blessed are," followed by a description of a group of people (for example, the poor in spirit, those who mourn, and so forth). We will immediately notice that the people Jesus is describing do not *seem* to be experiencing blessing. How is someone who is mourning *blessed*? How is someone who is persecuted and insulted *blessed*? It may be helpful to consider the meaning of the word "blessed" in the context of a beatitude.

Our first instinct is to equate beatitude (or "blessedness") with happiness, and there is some biblical basis for this. For example, the Good News Translation (GNT), which attempts to translate the Bible's Hebrew and Greek into the simplest, most accessible English possible, translates the word "blessed" in a biblical beatitude as "happy." The beginning of Psalm 1 appears in the New American Bible, Revised Edition (NABRE) as:

Blessed is the man who does not walk
　in the counsel of the wicked,
Nor stand in the way of sinners,
　nor sit in company with scoffers.

But in the Good News Translation (GNT), it is translated as:

Happy are those
　who reject the advice of evil people,
　who do not follow the example of sinners
　or join those who have no use for God.

Jesus' first beatitude in Matthew's Sermon on the Mount (5:3) appears this way in the NABRE:

"Blessed are the poor in spirit,
　for theirs is the kingdom of heaven."

In the GNT, "blessed" appears once again as "happy":

"Happy are those who know they
　are spiritually poor;
　the Kingdom of heaven belongs to them!"

Is there an important difference between being blessed and being happy? The difference worth stressing lies in the baleful circumstances of those whom Jesus calls blessed. From the poor ("in spirit"—more on that later) to the persecuted, those whom Jesus calls blessed do not seem to have much reason to be happy.

Happiness has long been associated with the American dream. Thomas Jefferson enshrined the pursuit of happiness in the Declaration of Independence as an "unalienable right" bestowed on all humankind by our Creator. Today, people still regard happiness as one of the ultimate goals in life. In the Beatitudes, Jesus takes a very different tack. While happiness may eventually arise from being blessed, it is the *un*happy circumstances that Jesus calls his disciples and the crowd to embrace that bring forth a blessed state. It is when they become the object of the world's disdain and its efforts to prevent them from being happy that they are given God's special blessings.

All across the United States, following the most casual daily greetings, we are often invited to "have a good day" or "have a nice day." In America's southern states, however, it is not uncommon for complete strangers to tell each other to "have a blessed day." When someone is asked how they are doing, it is common to hear the response, "I'm blessed."

These blessings are a sure sign that somewhere in their cultural DNA, these Americans have been influenced by churchgoers.

Having spent most of my life outside the south, I was initially surprised by the frequency of being blessed by strangers—convenience store clerks, cab drivers, and once even a police officer. The surprise of it set me to thinking, *What is the difference between having a nice day and having a blessed day?* It occurred to me that it was entirely possible to have a blessed day when the day was not at all nice. A blessed day is one in which you are aware of God's presence even if things are not going well. If you have faith that God is present in your day, you will be blessed with the courage and strength to meet the challenges of that day, whatever they may be.

Jesus' assurance that certain people in difficult circumstances are blessed does not imply that they are necessarily happy in their circumstances or that they are supposed to feel happy. But it does mean that God is with them. God has taken account of them and will not let anything that is causing them to suffer take them away from God's care. Knowing this might not lead to immediate happiness, but it can fill one's spirit with sufficient hope to carry on.

 Matthew favors the **mountain** as the site for divine revelation. Not only does the Sermon on the Mount take place on a mountain but also the transfiguration (17:1) and the Great Commission (28:16). Jesus also goes to the mountain to pray (14:23) and to heal (15:29). The Bible views mountains as holy sites, close to God. (See also Moses receiving the Torah in Exod 24:12-18.)

If there is a key to interpreting the Beatitudes, it is understanding the meaning of the phrase "kingdom of heaven." In order to understand this phrase, we can look to Jesus' parables about the kingdom of heaven. The parables announce the nearness of the kingdom of heaven. In fact, they tell those who listen carefully that the kingdom is not just nearby, it is available for entry by those who understand its value and are willing to pay the "entry fee." How expensive is the kingdom of heaven?

> "The kingdom of heaven is like a treasure buried in a field, which a person finds and hides again, and out of joy goes and sells all that he has and buys that field. Again, the kingdom of heaven is like a merchant searching for fine pearls. When he finds a pearl of great price, he goes and sells all that he has and buys it." (Matt 13:44-46)

Indeed, whatever we value more than the kingdom is what we have to surrender in order to gain admittance. And ultimately, it is Jesus himself who is the key that opens the way to the kingdom.

> "Whoever loves father or mother more than me is not worthy of me, and whoever loves son or daughter more than me is not worthy of me; and whoever does not take up his cross and follow after me is not worthy of me. Whoever finds his life will lose it, and whoever loses his life for my sake will find it." (Matt 10:37-39)

In his parables, Jesus proclaims the nearness (the "at-handedness") of the kingdom of heaven. In the Beatitudes, he identifies those who are promised entry into that kingdom. Their assured entry is not simply a promise of pie-in-the-sky after they die. The kingdom of heaven is not to be confused with going to heaven, although the heaven that awaits the blessed is certainly part of the concept of the kingdom of heaven. The kingdom of heaven that Jesus announces is to be understood, first of all, as the realm in which God's authority is exercised without limitation, and Jesus announces its availability to those who are willing to accept God's rule in their earthly lives.

In his preaching and through his powerful works of healing and forgiveness, Jesus gives witness to the truth that the kingdom of heaven

> **The Beatitudes**
>
> [3]"Blessed are the poor in spirit,
>   for theirs is the kingdom of heaven.
> [4]Blessed are they who mourn,
>   for they will be comforted.
>
> *continue*

can be entered now. The Beatitudes and the entire Sermon on the Mount make it perfectly clear, however, that to enter the kingdom of heaven in the present also means becoming a prophetic agent of the kingdom. The disciples who would enter the kingdom now must proclaim in word and deed and in every aspect of their daily lives that the kingdom is both a present reality as well as an event yet to transpire in its fullness.

The Poor in Spirit (5:3)

In the first beatitude of the Sermon on the Mount, Jesus blesses "the poor *in spirit*," while in Luke's version (known as the Sermon on the Plain), Jesus blesses "the poor" (Luke 6:20). Luke's gospel is noted for its emphasis on the poor, mentioning them far more often than any other gospel does. Jesus' blessing of the poor in the Sermon on the Plain is only the second explicit mention of the poor in Luke. The first mention is in his proclamation of Isaiah 61:1-2 in the synagogue at Nazareth: "The Spirit of the Lord is upon me, / because he has anointed me / to bring glad tidings to the poor" (Luke 4:18). The poor are always a focus of God's concern. Care for the poor is embedded in the law of Moses. For example, in Leviticus we read, "[Y]ou shall not pick your vineyard bare, nor gather up the grapes that have fallen. These things you shall leave for the poor and the alien. I, the LORD, am your God" (19:10). And in Deuteronomy 15:11 it is written: "The land will never lack for needy persons; that is why I command you: 'Open your hand freely to your poor and to your needy kin in your land.'"

Is there a difference between "the poor" in Luke and "the poor in spirit" in Matthew? If

being poor is to be equated with poverty—that is, having insufficient access to the goods required to reasonably sustain a modest but respectable life in a given society—then there may well be a difference between being poor and being poor in spirit. That would define being poor by what can be objectively observed about one's living conditions. But the *experience* of being poor may well be something that is shared by those who are poor and those who are poor in spirit.

In the religious milieu of the Israelites of Jesus' day, being poor meant being acutely aware that what one needs in life is not guaranteed from one day to the next. Being poor meant living from hand to mouth, never knowing if the needs of the next day could be sufficiently met. If you can't rely on yourself or others to meet your basic needs (and the needs of your family), whom can you rely on? You rely upon God, you trust in God, and you hope in God. This reliance on God is more than wanting God to provide for your needs—it is knowing that it is God whom you need most of all. And this is what is meant by being "poor in spirit"—knowing that you are a needy person and that your greatest need is God. So it is possible to be poor in spirit without living in poverty, but the physically poor are more likely also to be poor in spirit.

The first beatitude of the Sermon on the Mount tells us that there is a blessedness to this condition. We hear something of that blessedness in the peacefulness expressed by the psalmist: "In peace I will lie down and fall asleep, / for you alone, LORD, make me secure" (Ps 4:9).

To know the blessedness of being utterly dependent upon God is to experience God's personal care, and, according to Jesus, those who experience God's personal care have already gained entrance into the kingdom of heaven.

Those Who Mourn (5:4)

Mourning is always painful. Thus the second beatitude underscores the need to distinguish between being happy and being blessed.

When we reflect on our own times of mourning we are reminded of those loved ones who have died and the grief experienced in losing them. Where is the blessing in that? Faith and hope both assure us that our loss is temporary and that those who have died in Christ have gained everything.

In blessing those who mourn, however, Jesus likely has a wider, more communal lens in mind. He is probably blessing those who collectively mourn for Israel. Recall, for example, the heartfelt mourning of Psalm 80:

> LORD of hosts,
>   how long will you smolder in anger
>   while your people pray?
> You have fed them the bread of tears,
>   made them drink tears in great measure.
> You have left us to be fought over by our
>   neighbors;
>   our enemies deride us.
> O God of hosts, restore us;
>   light up your face and we shall be saved.
>   (Ps 80:5-8)

As in all the beatitudes and directives of the Sermon on the Mount, it is Jesus himself who lives them most fully and so provides us with the prime example to follow. Although it may seem impossible to imitate Jesus in all things, if we are to be disciples, that must always be our goal—a goal that remains with us in spite of any and all of our failures.

Jesus provides us with an example of mourning for Israel in Matthew 23:37:

> "Jerusalem, Jerusalem, you who kill the prophets and stone those sent to you, how many times I yearned to gather your children together, as a hen gathers her young under her wings, but you were unwilling!"

We are given a fuller picture of Jesus mourning for Jerusalem in Luke 19:41-43:

> As he drew near, he saw the city and wept over it, saying, "If this day you only knew what makes for peace—but now it is hidden from your eyes. For the days are coming upon you when your enemies will raise a palisade against you; they will encircle you and hem you in on all sides."

And as he carries his cross to meet his death, Jesus warns the women weeping for him to weep instead for themselves and for their own children:

> A large crowd of people followed Jesus, including many women who mourned and lamented him. Jesus turned to them and said, "Daughters of Jerusalem, do not weep for me; weep instead for yourselves and for your children, for indeed, the days are coming when people will say, 'Blessed are the barren, the wombs that never bore and the breasts that never nursed.' At that time people will say to the mountains, 'Fall upon us!' and to the hills, 'Cover us!' for if these things are done when the wood is green what will happen when it is dry?" (Luke 23:27-31)

Jesus not only blesses mourners because of the woes that are about to befall the nation due to Israel's ensuing rebellion against the Roman overlords (AD 66–73); he is also blessing the nation's grief over the absence of God's rule in Israel. There was a cherished belief prior to 587 BC that the rule of King David and his heirs reflected an eternal covenant between God and Israel (primarily the tribe of Judah). This covenant with the Davidic line was expressed by God through the prophet Nathan in the Second Book of Samuel:

> Thus says the LORD of hosts: I took you from the pasture, from following the flock, to become ruler over my people Israel. . . . Moreover, the LORD also declares to you that the LORD will make a house for you: when your days have been completed and you rest with your ancestors, I will raise up your offspring after you, sprung from your loins, and I will establish his kingdom. He it is who shall build a house for my name, and I will establish his royal throne forever. (7:8, 11-13)

It should be noted that this "eternal" covenant came with a caveat concerning any heir to David's throne: "If he does wrong, I will reprove him with a human rod and with human

> ⁵Blessed are the meek,
>   for they will inherit the land.
>
> *continue*

punishments" (2 Sam 7:14b). Nevertheless, it was the firm belief of the religious and royal establishment of Israel that God was the true king of Israel (Judah) and that God ruled through the heir to David's throne, who was considered to be the adopted son of God.

Many of the Royal Psalms that are considered messianic in the Christian tradition were originally prayers for the kings of Judah, descendants of David. Of special interest is Psalm 2:

"I myself have installed my king
    on Zion, my holy mountain."
I will proclaim the decree of the LORD,
    he said to me, "You are my son;
    today I have begotten you.
Ask it of me,
    and I will give you the nations as your
        inheritance,
    and, as your possession, the ends of the earth.
With an iron rod you will shepherd them,
    like a potter's vessel you will shatter them."
        (Ps 2:6-9)

Theologically, this meant that Judah, under the rule of the Davidic kings, was considered to be the kingdom of God.

In 587 BC Babylon conquered Judah, destroyed the temple, and drove the skilled inhabitants into exile in Babylon. An heir of David would never again rule over an Israelite (or Jewish) nation. Amazingly, this did not bring an end to the people's trust in God's covenant with David. Instead, for many, it transformed it. The tragic end of the Davidic dynasty brought about an entirely new understanding of what it would mean to be "the kingdom of God" and how and when an heir to David would reestablish that kingdom.

Thus Jesus' proclamation that the kingdom of God (or the kingdom of heaven) was at hand would have been the most exciting claim imaginable. Ironically, the second beatitude assured Jesus' disciples—and any in the crowds who were willing to hear it—that the blessing of the kingdom was for those who desired it so much that they mourned its absence in Israel. The comfort of mourners lies in knowing that their yearning for the kingdom opens them to participation in that kingdom.

After two thousand years, this is an important beatitude for us as well. We are not called to mourn the absence of an ancient royal dynasty in Israel—after all, we are among the people who have welcomed the Messiah. We believe he reigns over the kingdom of heaven from heaven itself. But we are still expected to mourn because God's will is not done on earth as it is in heaven. Wherever we see or hear of injustice, violence, disease, famine, poverty, or any physical or spiritual ill, we are expected to grieve the separation of the world from God. Such mourning is meant to increase our compassionate efforts to stand in the gap and address the gulf.

The Meek (5:5)

Many translations adopt a wider view of the inheritance of the meek in the third beatitude. In step with the King James Bible and the Revised Standard Version, the New Revised Standard Version states, "Blessed are the meek, for they will inherit the earth." Both *land* and *earth* are perfectly acceptable translations. Nevertheless, *land* probably more correctly identifies what Jesus intended. This is because the Beatitudes are the blessings of those who are on their way to inheriting the kingdom, and the kingdom was thought to encompass the land promised to Abraham and his descendants—the Promised Land.

Why the meek? Why are they going to inherit the land? Many in Israel were growing in the certainty that the long-awaited divinely governed kingdom could only come about through violence. This certainty would erupt in an attempted revolution that finally led the Romans to crush the Jewish revolt and destroy the Temple in AD 70. This kind of political tension and upheaval is why we hear Jesus saying,

"From the days of John the Baptist until now, the kingdom of heaven suffers violence, and the violent are taking it by force" (Matt 11:12).

Throughout the gospels of the New Testament we encounter Jesus eschewing violence. This is perhaps most poignantly demonstrated in the Gospel of John when Pilate interrogates Jesus concerning his role as king:

> Jesus answered, "My kingdom does not belong to this world. If my kingdom did belong to this world, my attendants [would] be fighting to keep me from being handed over to the Jews. But as it is, my kingdom is not here." (John 18:36)

To understand what being meek meant to Jesus, we must contemplate Jesus as the essential example of meekness:

> "Come to me, all you who labor and are burdened, and I will give you rest. Take my yoke upon you and learn from me, for I am meek and humble of heart; and you will find rest for yourselves. For my yoke is easy, and my burden light." (Matt 11:28-30)

Being meek does not mean being passive in the face of evil. It means to resist evil peacefully. Jesus, meek and humble of heart, went about doing good in the face of organized opposition with such determination that it led to his execution on a cross as an enemy of both political and religious authorities. Meek is not weak, nor is it bare fisted. It is gloved in the hand of God.

Meekness is humility. It is the virtue possessed by those who trust in God rather than in their own powers. Humility is not the denial or rejection of one's own powers or abilities. Being meek means to yoke one's powers to the one who gave them to us in the first place.

Those Who Hunger and Thirst for Righteousness (5:6)

We often think of righteousness as a synonym for holiness. Understood this way, righteousness has very strong religious connotations. A righteous person might be said to

> [6]Blessed are they who hunger and thirst for righteousness,
>   for they will be satisfied.
>
> *continue*

live a "godly" life, avoiding immorality and exhibiting commitment to frequent worship and prayer. But holiness is not the best synonym for righteousness. Holiness, in its biblical context, means to be set apart for God in some special way.

In both the Old and New Testaments, righteousness is understood in the context of the covenant relationship with God. Living according to God's will or God's law puts the people or an individual in right relationship with God and with each other. Another definition of the word most commonly translated into English as "righteous" is the term "just." Those who hunger and thirst for righteousness are not so much seeking holiness as they are desiring justice.

There are two aspects to the fourth beatitude. First, Jesus blesses those who hunger and thirst to be righteous themselves. To hunger and thirst for personal righteousness brings to mind the third beatitude. This kind of hunger is surely akin to mourning. It is the regret for one's own sinfulness, for one's failure to live and act justly toward others, that leads to repentance and forgiveness. To be forgiven is to be truly blessed. But there is also the greater sense of this beatitude: the deep desire to see a world broken by injustice, violence, greed—the list goes on and on—repaired and set right as it will be when God's will finally prevails and all creation becomes fully part of the kingdom of heaven.

What a bold promise it is, that those who yearn for a world filled with righteousness from mountain tops to ocean depths will contemplate the world and be satisfied that there is only justice, that nowhere is there turmoil, war, or violence, only peace and goodwill. As with all the Beatitudes, however, this is not just

> [7]Blessed are the merciful,
>   for they will be shown mercy.
> [8]Blessed are the clean of heart,
>   for they will see God.
>
> *continue*

a promise but a directive. Those who hunger and thirst are always searching for food and drink. Those who hunger and thirst for righteousness must always seek to bring it about.

The Merciful (5:7)

In announcing the special Holy Year of Mercy (which began on December 8, 2015), Pope Francis proclaimed: "Jesus Christ is the face of the Father's mercy. These words might well sum up the mystery of the Christian faith. Mercy has become living and visible in Jesus of Nazareth, reaching its culmination in him." Strangely enough, the beatitude found in Matthew 5:7 might lead us to the mistaken belief that we have to show mercy to others before God will be merciful to us. Pope Francis reminds us that God is the source of all mercy, most especially in his Son Jesus Christ. God's mercy, "living and visible," is always available to us.

Being recipients of God's compassionate love, we are free to make mercy the motivating force behind our relationship with others—with *all* others. In that way we are also assured of God's continued mercy. Fr. Frank Matera, in his splendid volume *The Sermon on the Mount: The Perfect Measure of the Christian Life*, summarizes the fifth beatitude by saying, "Those who are merciful are those who know that God is merciful, and so they are merciful to others."

In Matthew 18:21-35, the parable of the Unforgiving Servant, Jesus dramatically affirms that it is the experience of receiving mercy that requires us to show mercy in return. In this parable a servant who is forgiven a huge debt but shows no mercy to a fellow servant who owes him only a small debt ends up being handed over to torturers until he repays the debt that was once forgiven him. This parable warns against any possibility of thinking we can accept God's mercy and then fail to be merciful to others.

In an ancient homily on the fifth beatitude, St. John Chrysostom asserts that this beatitude does not imply a simple reciprocity, a tit-for-tat, God showing us mercy because we have shown mercy to others. There is no equating God's mercy with our mercy. We understand this best when we consider that God's mercy is to receive us into eternal life, to grant us a full share in Christ's resurrection. Our acts of mercy, as important as they are, pale in comparison.

The overwhelming nature of God's mercy should indeed overwhelm us, turning our lives into opportunities to show God's mercy to everyone we encounter, whether our exchanges with others seem insignificant or life-altering.

The Clean of Heart (5:8)

As I write about this beatitude, I feel compelled to acknowledge the challenge that Jesus' words pose to me personally. Being clean or pure of heart seems an insurmountable spiritual hurdle to me. I want to see God, but there is a lot of clutter in my heart. Philosopher Søren Kierkegaard (1813–1855) asserted that purity of heart is to will one thing. But if you look into his story, you realize he wasn't very good at that. Neither am I. Day in and day out, the objects of my will can be extremely trivial, focusing one moment on a cup of coffee and on to a spoonful of yogurt the next. And then there are worse things I also tend toward. My heart is like a dog in a forest full of squirrels!

I am reminded of the prayerful words of the poet and Anglican priest John Donne, whose life straddled the sixteenth and seventeenth centuries. He knew well Augustine's desire to be "chaste—but not yet":

> Batter my heart, three-person'd God, for you
>   As yet but knock, breathe, shine, and seek to
>   mend;

That I may rise and stand, o'erthrow me, and
   bend
Your force to break, blow, burn, and make me
   new.
I, like an usurp'd town to another due,
Labor to admit you, but oh, to no end;
Reason, your viceroy in me, me should defend,
But is captiv'd, and proves weak or untrue.
Yet dearly I love you, and would be lov'd fain,
But am betroth'd unto your enemy;
Divorce me, untie or break that knot again,
Take me to you, imprison me, for I,
Except you enthrall me, never shall be free,
Nor ever chaste, except you ravish me.
(Holy Sonnet 14)

In both the Gospel of John (1:18) and the First Letter of John (4:12), we are told that no one has ever seen God. In John 14, shortly before his arrest and crucifixion, Jesus warns his disciples that he is going away. Philip (perhaps because he is pure of heart) deeply desires one last thing from Jesus. He wants Jesus to show him the Father. Jesus' response tells us everything we need to know about seeing the Father:

Jesus said to him, "Have I been with you for so long a time and you still do not know me, Philip? Whoever has seen me has seen the Father. How can you say, 'Show us the Father'?" (John 14:9)

I can see Jesus in the gospels. At Eucharist I attempt to attend fully to his presence and his gift of himself to me, but my attempts always remind me of how cluttered my heart is. Yet I am deeply reassured by Jesus' reply to Philip. Jesus shows us the Father by revealing himself to us in word and sacrament, and so in some mysterious fashion, Jesus must be trying to make our hearts pure at the same time. The more clearly we can see Jesus, the more clearly we can see God.

Remembering that God appeared to Moses in a flaming bush without consuming it, perhaps it is worth asking God to set our hearts afire, consuming everything but the pure, clean desire to be a home for God: "A clean heart create for me, God; / renew within me a steadfast spirit" (Ps 51:12).

> [9]Blessed are the peacemakers,
>   for they will be called children of God.
>
> *continue*

The Peacemakers (5:9)

It seems that history itself is seldom more than a recounting of human violence. Every civilization could be remembered most of all for the wars it fought, won, and lost. Even Jesus warns us not to interpret the news of wars as a sign of the end. We will always have wars, but they are not the end of the world:

As he was sitting on the Mount of Olives, the disciples approached him privately and said, "Tell us . . . what sign will there be of your coming, and of the end of the age?" Jesus said to them in reply, "See that no one deceives you. For many will come in my name, saying, 'I am the Messiah,' and they will deceive many. You will hear of wars and reports of wars; see that you are not alarmed, for these things must happen, but it will not yet be the end." (Matt 24:3-6)

America's wars during its brief (by world standards) history provide no relief from the perception that historical chronicles chiefly involve the shedding of blood. This begs the question, who have been the peacemakers? Who in our history can we recall that are worthy of being called the children of God?

Let's take a closer look. Every time a mother brings a halt to a fight between siblings, they have encountered a peacemaker. When a counselor helps resolve the bitter tension between spouses that have not yet completely forgotten how to love each other, the work of peacemaking has been achieved. When some brave soul offers to mediate in a civil or legal dispute, a peacemaker is present.

There will be wars and rumors of wars, but how many wars have been avoided because of the courageous work of peacemakers? It could be that peacemakers, whether they know it or not, are doing the work of God by simply seeking peace and not the limelight of historical remembrance. And there have been truly noteworthy historical events of peacemaking: the Camp David Accords that brought peace between Egypt and Israel in 1978, the Strategic Arms Limitation Talks that helped prevent nuclear war between the US and the Soviet Union, and, in the twenty-first century, the valiant attempts to bring peace to a civil war raging for over fifty years in Colombia between the government and the FARC rebels. Peacemakers are not always successful. Sometimes they are successful only for brief periods of time. Calling these peacemakers children of God, however, is never an error. It simply corroborates what Jesus says of them.

When Jesus spoke of peace, he would have had in mind the Hebrew word *shalom*, a rich word with deep roots in the Old Testament. *Shalom* implies far more than an absence of violence or turmoil. It is the peace of good health, the peace of prosperity, and the peace of wholeness. In calling his disciples to be peacemakers, Jesus is calling them to bring to others what Jesus said he came to bring to them: "I came so that they might have life and have it more abundantly" (John 10:10b).

Jesus also says:

> "Peace I leave with you; my peace I give to you. Not as the world gives do I give it to you. Do not let your hearts be troubled or afraid. You heard me tell you, 'I am going away and I will come back to you.' If you loved me, you would rejoice that I am going to the Father; for the Father is greater than I." (John 14:27-28)

The peace Jesus gives to his disciples is not like any peace that may be found in the current order of the world. Jesus is giving his disciples the peace the Son enjoys in the presence of the Father. He is leaving them behind, but they now share in his ultimate peace.

In Matthew this special peace is the peace associated with the kingdom of heaven. We see this most clearly in Matthew 10:5-13, when Jesus names his twelve apostles and sends them out to proclaim the gospel of the kingdom:

> Jesus sent out these twelve after instructing them thus, "Do not go into pagan territory or enter a Samaritan town. Go rather to the lost sheep of the house of Israel. As you go, make this proclamation: 'The kingdom of heaven is at hand.' Cure the sick, raise the dead, cleanse lepers, drive out demons. Without cost you have received; without cost you are to give. Do not take gold or silver or copper for your belts; no sack for the journey, or a second tunic, or sandals, or walking stick. The laborer deserves his keep. Whatever town or village you enter, look for a worthy person in it, and stay there until you leave. As you enter a house, wish it peace. If the house is worthy, let your peace come upon it; if not, let your peace return to you."

This passage reinforces the message that when we hear or read the Beatitudes, we are to remember that these are blessings to be found in the kingdom of heaven and that the kingdom of heaven is at hand. Being a peacemaker is about proclaiming the Good News of the kingdom—the realm where the peace of Christ reigns over all. This is the great significance of sharing the sign of peace during Mass. It is much more than an opportunity to smile at your fellow parishioner. It is the power granted you by Christ to extend the peace of the kingdom of God to one another.

Despite the close association between peace and the kingdom of heaven, in both Matthew and Luke Jesus warns that his mission is not to bring peace, but division.

> "Do not think that I have come to bring peace upon the earth. I have come to bring not peace but the sword. For I have come to set / a man 'against his father, / a daughter against her mother, / and a daughter-in-law against her mother-in-law; / and one's enemies will be those of his household.'" (Matt 10:34-36; see Luke 12:51-53)

Following Christ will inevitably create divisions within households, but in no sense are

Jesus' warnings meant to suggest that his followers would deliberately choose to become enemies of their own families. How Jesus' followers are to deal with those who turn against them will be made abundantly clear later in the Sermon on the Mount (Matt 5:38-48).

The Persecuted (5:10, 11-12)

The eighth beatitude seems very much like the ninth—so much so that many count only eight beatitudes, viewing the ninth as an elaboration of the eighth:

> "Blessed are you when they insult you and persecute you and utter every kind of evil against you [falsely] because of me. Rejoice and be glad, for your reward will be great in heaven. Thus they persecuted the prophets who were before you." (Matt 5:11-12)

There are key differences that warrant considering these to be two different, albeit similar, beatitudes. The eighth beatitude, like all the previous beatitudes in Matthew's Sermon on the Mount, is stated in the third person plural: "Blessed are they." As such, it could be a blessing on anyone or any group of people that meet the conditions of the blessing. In the ninth beatitude the blessing becomes personal and specific to those who hear him proclaim it: "Blessed are you."

> [10]Blessed are they who are persecuted for the sake of righteousness,
> for theirs is the kingdom of heaven.
>
> [11]Blessed are you when they insult you and persecute you and utter every kind of evil against you [falsely] because of me. [12]Rejoice and be glad, for your reward will be great in heaven. Thus they persecuted the prophets who were before you.

The other difference between these two beatitudes is found in the causes of persecution. In the eighth beatitude, those who commit themselves to righteousness are persecuted. In the ninth, "you" who are associated with Jesus are persecuted. It is quite possible, of course, that the righteous who are persecuted are righteous because of their commitment to following Jesus. In Matthew 25, however, it becomes clear that there are those who will be counted among the righteous who were not aware of their association with Jesus. It is enough to act justly toward Jesus' followers to be counted among the righteous:

> "When the Son of Man comes in his glory, and all the angels with him, he will sit upon his

 The US bishops noted the importance of the Beatitudes in implementing **economic justice for all people** in their pastoral letter on the topic:

> We write to share our teaching, to raise questions, to challenge one another to live our faith in the world. We write as heirs of the biblical prophets who summon us "to do the right and to love goodness, and to walk humbly with your God" (Mic 6:8). We write as followers of Jesus who told us in the Sermon on the Mount: "Blessed are the poor in spirit . . . Blessed are the meek . . . Blessed are they who hunger and thirst for righteousness . . . You are the salt of the earth . . . You are the light of the world" (Matt 5:1-6, 13-14). These words challenge us not only as believers but also as consumers, citizens, workers, and owners. In the parable of the Last Judgment, Jesus said, "For I was hungry and you gave me food, I was thirsty and you gave me drink . . . As often as you did it for one of my least brothers, you did it for me" (Matt 25:35-40). The challenge for us is to discover in our own place and time what it means to be "poor in spirit" and "the salt of the earth" and what it means to serve "the least among us" and to "hunger and thirst for righteousness." (*Economic Justice for All*, 4)

glorious throne, and all the nations will be assembled before him. And he will separate them one from another, as a shepherd separates the sheep from the goats. He will place the sheep on his right and the goats on his left. Then the king will say to those on his right, 'Come, you who are blessed by my Father. Inherit the kingdom prepared for you from the foundation of the world. For I was hungry and you gave me food, I was thirsty and you gave me drink, a stranger and you welcomed me, naked and you clothed me, ill and you cared for me, in prison and you visited me.' Then the righteous will answer him and say, 'Lord, when did we see you hungry and feed you, or thirsty and give you drink? When did we see you a stranger and welcome you, or naked and clothe you? When did we see you ill or in prison, and visit you?' And the king will say to them in reply, 'Amen, I say to you, whatever you did for one of these least brothers of mine, you did for me.'" (Matt 25:31-40)

Read or heard together, the Beatitudes are a singular blessing of those who commit to being Jesus' disciples. The blessing is the assurance that they have already begun life in the kingdom of heaven. This is the case even if their lives end in pain and suffering at the hands of others in acts of persecution. Whatever woes Jesus' followers experience in life cannot remove them from the blessed state into which they have been invited by Jesus. At Jesus' arrest and crucifixion this truth will be too much for his disciples to comprehend, let alone believe. But after the resurrection they will come to believe that Jesus himself is the ultimate example of a life lived according to the beatitudes he taught.

EXPLORING LESSON ONE

1. a) What are the two different groups Jesus addresses in the Sermon on the Mount, and how do they differ from each other (5:1-2)?

The disciples and the crowd following Jesus. He teaches the disciples and expects them (us) to live the Beautitudes.

b) What is the significance of Jesus sitting down to teach (5:1-2)?

The normal position of a teacher.

2. When used today, what differences in meaning do you sense between the words *blessed* and *happy*?

Blessed — given grace

Happy - joyful

3. In the Sermon on the Mount, Jesus blesses the "poor in spirit" (5:3) and not simply "the poor" as in the Sermon on the Plain (Luke 6:20). What does it mean to be poor in spirit?

To be aware of an emptiness — to yearn for God — to be aware that we are gift and to be given away.

4. In its original context, the beatitude blessing mourners (5:4) was connected to a deep desire for God's kingdom. When have you mourned the condition of society, desiring God's intervention?

Almost daily — w/ mass shootings, wars, hate speech, the divisiveness of the political landscape, the lies, & misinformation, the name calling

5. What does meekness mean to you? How does the commentary's explanation of meekness challenge or confirm any previous understanding you may have had of meekness (5:5)?

_____

_____

_____

_____

6. What are the two ways of understanding the beatitude about hungering and thirsting for righteousness (5:6), according to the commentary? Which one resonates with you the most?

① Someone living a godly life in prayer & relationship
② Anyone who is seeking justice in the world —
Seeking to ROOT out injustice & seeks the
kingdom

7. What are some practical acts of mercy that many of us might aspire to perform on a daily or regular basis (5:7)?

To NOT Gossip or judge others
To allow others to be themselves w/o judging

_____

_____

8. In your own words, what do you think it means to have a clean (or pure) heart (5:8)?

A heart that seeks to do what Jesus
would do.

_____

_____

_____

9. In what areas of daily life can a person without significant influence on society still act as a peacemaker (5:9), and what wider impact could these efforts eventually have?

Stop judging; be merciful.

_____

_____

_____

_____

10. a) Where and when have you witnessed or experienced persecution "for the sake of righteousness" (5:10)?

_____

_____

_____

    b) Where are followers of Christ persecuted today (5:11)? What can be done for them?

_____

_____

_____

CLOSING PRAYER

Prayer

He began to teach them . . .   (Matt 5:2)

You are the authoritative teacher, Lord Jesus. Your words have power because you lived what you taught. Make room in us to truly listen to your teaching so that our lives will be an authentic and persuasive witness to the kingdom you proclaimed. We pray for all those who have taught us to turn to you, our teachers and mentors, especially . . .

LESSON TWO

Matthew 5:13-48

Begin your personal study and group discussion with a simple and sincere prayer such as:

Prayer

Jesus, you teach us to listen to your words and imitate your deeds. Be with me now as I listen for your voice, and help me to become more like you.

Read the Bible text of Matthew 5:13-48 found in the outside columns of pages 30–39, highlighting what stands out to you.

Read the accompanying commentary to add to your understanding.

Respond to the questions on pages 41–42, Exploring Lesson Two.

The Closing Prayer on page 43 is for your personal use and may be used at the end of group discussion.

The Similes of Salt and Light

¹³"You are the salt of the earth. But if salt loses its taste, with what can it be seasoned? It is no longer good for anything but to be thrown out and trampled underfoot. ¹⁴You are the light of the world. A city set on a mountain cannot be hidden. ¹⁵Nor do they light a lamp and then put it under a bushel basket; it is set on a lampstand, where it gives light to all in the house. ¹⁶Just so, your light must shine before others, that they may see your good deeds and glorify your heavenly Father.

continue

5:13-48 "BUT I SAY TO YOU . . ."

Salt and Light (5:13-16)

"Preach the Gospel without ceasing, and if necessary, use words." This directive traditionally attributed to St. Francis of Assisi captures much of the intent of what Jesus tells his disciples in Matthew 5:13-16. If we are followers of Christ, the manner in which we live our lives will be our most important witness to the world. We are called to be the salt of the earth and the light of the world. But are we what we are called to be? If the message of the Gospel is to be believed by others, it has to be lived by us. Salt must be savory, and light must be bright.

Probing deeper into what Jesus says about salt losing its taste (5:13) has puzzled many through the ages. How can salt lose its flavor? Said in a positive way, the statement that "salt must be savory if it is to truly be salt" tells us what is most important. Being the salt of the earth means living a life that adds real value to the lives we encounter.

Nevertheless, our natural curiosity leads us to wonder if salt can actually lose its saltiness. And if it can, as Jesus asks, what can "season" it (literally "salt" it) to make it salty again? Some have suggested that much of the salt in Jesus' day would have been gathered from the shores of the Dead Sea (which is extremely salty) but that it would be impure, mixed up with all sorts of things also found on the shore. This salt would be used by a family until nothing remained of it but the impurities that would no longer be of any value as salt. This remaining portion would simply be tossed out and ground underfoot by passersby.

Another theory which has grown in favor of late is that Jesus is referring to the salt that bakers may have used to line the bottom of their ovens. Some Arab bakers in the Middle East today apparently still line their outdoor ovens with salt, which acts as a catalyst in baking. The catalytic qualities of the salt eventually diminish, and the salt is then disposed of for having lost its purpose. In either theory, there is little that can be done to make the remaining salt salty again.

The real question, however, is not how salt can lose its saltiness, but how do we remain the salt of the earth? How do disciples make their lives and their message so savory, so preservative, that the world at large is not only attracted to but benefits from their presence? Answering these questions is simple—it's a matter of fully embracing what Jesus teaches. But putting this into practice is not so simple. Perhaps we will be well on our way by considering how disciples are to be the light of the world.

What activities make Christ's disciples "light" (5:14-16)? They certainly aren't public displays of piety. "When you pray," Jesus will tell his disciples later in the sermon, "go to your inner room, close the door, and pray to your Father in secret" (6:6). In Matthew 23:5 Jesus criticizes the scribes and the Pharisees because "[a]ll their works are performed to be seen." A city on a mountain top and a lamp on a lampstand are supposed to be seen. What are the good deeds the disciples are to put on public display, and how do they avoid the hypocrisy Jesus denounces in the scribes and Pharisees?

Earlier in the gospel, as Jesus proclaimed the good news of the kingdom of heaven, he made its reality known through both his teachings and his actions. Matthew tells us that when John the Baptist was in prison, he sought reassurance that Jesus was in fact the Messiah. He sent some of his own disciples to Jesus to ask him, "Are you the one who is to come, or should we look for another?" (Matt 11:3). In response, Jesus tells John's disciples that his deeds are proof that he is the one who is making the kingdom of heaven a manifest reality: "Go and tell John what you hear and see: the blind regain their sight, the lame walk, lepers are cleansed, the deaf hear, the dead are raised, and the poor have the good news proclaimed to them. And blessed is the one who takes no offense at me" (Matt 11:4-6).

Earlier in Matthew, when Jesus sent out the Twelve to further his own mission to proclaim the Gospel of the kingdom, Jesus gave them this commission: "As you go, make this proclamation: 'The kingdom of heaven is at hand.' Cure the sick, raise the dead, cleanse lepers, drive out demons. Without cost you have received; without cost you are to give" (Matt 10:7-8). The good deeds that Jesus' disciples are to perform, which will make their light shine for all to see, are the same good deeds that Jesus himself performs in making the reality of the kingdom of heaven known. We are to be about the same tasks of caring for the poor, the disabled, the sick, and all who are in need. Indeed, if we perform these tasks faithfully, the world will see in the light we bring

---

Teaching about the Law

[17]"Do not think that I have come to abolish the law or the prophets. I have come not to abolish but to fulfill. [18]Amen, I say to you, until heaven and earth pass away, not the smallest letter or the smallest part of a letter will pass from the law, until all things have taken place. [19]Therefore, whoever breaks one of the least of these commandments and teaches others to do so will be called least in the kingdom of heaven. But whoever obeys and teaches these commandments will be called greatest in the kingdom of heaven. [20]I tell you, unless your righteousness surpasses that of the scribes and Pharisees, you will not enter into the kingdom of heaven.

continue

---

that Jesus is present, and we will bring flavor to the world.

Teaching about the Law (5:17-20)

It is at this juncture in the Sermon on the Mount that Matthew presents one of the most theologically difficult themes of his gospel: Jesus' teaching about the law of Moses. As Christians, we typically adopt the view that the Mosaic Law (including circumcision, food laws, and other external practices) is no longer in effect for those who have faith in Christ. This perspective can be found in Paul's letters (such as in Rom 10:4 or Gal 3:23-26).

For example, in the following passage about the reconciliation of Gentiles and Jews in Christ, Paul claims that the law has been abolished:

But now in Christ Jesus you who once were far off have become near by the blood of Christ.

For he is our peace, he who made both one and broke down the dividing wall of enmity, through his flesh, *abolishing the law with its commandments and legal claims*, that he might create in himself one new person in place of the two, thus establishing peace. (Eph 2:13-15; emphasis mine)

Christianity has generally adopted Paul's certainty that following Christ's death and resurrection, the Mosaic Law was replaced by faith in Christ. This is the basis for Gentile Christians entering a covenantal relationship with God: "[I]f you confess with your mouth that Jesus is Lord and believe in your heart that God raised him from the dead, you will be saved" (Rom 10:9). But we find something quite different at this point in Matthew's gospel:

> "Do not think that I have come to abolish the law or the prophets. I have come not to abolish but to fulfill. Amen, I say to you, until heaven and earth pass away, not the smallest letter or the smallest part of a letter will pass from the law, until all things have taken place." (Matt 5:17-18)

How are we to reconcile what Matthew tells us Jesus taught about the Mosaic Law and what Paul taught about the law? One factor to consider is the different audiences being addressed. Writing for a primarily *Gentile-Christian* audience, Paul is motivated to explain how believers are made righteous by faith in Christ rather than by the law (for example, Phil 3:9). Writing for a primarily *Jewish-Christian* audience, Matthew has reason to emphasize the ongoing value of the Mosaic Law in the lives of believers, stressing the continuity of God's revelation.

But how does Matthew understand what Jesus means when he says that he has come to "fulfill" the law and that no part of the law, however large or small, will pass away until heaven and earth pass away? Some suggest that "fulfilling" the law means that Jesus will keep the law perfectly himself, without ever deviating from it. These scholars tend to think that in the Sermon on the Mount, Jesus takes on a rabbinical role, teaching what is actually intended to be the living heart and ultimate intention of the law, and then living it out to the fullest. In this scenario, the historical Jesus never contemplated that his followers would ever be anything other than faithful Jews, continuing to live according to the Mosaic Law.

Other scholars suggest that Matthew understands Jesus' death and resurrection as an event that brings about a new heaven and a new earth. One of the more prominent scholars claiming this to be the case is John P. Meier. (See Suggested Reading list.) The assertion is made that by dying and rising from the dead, Jesus has fulfilled all that the law set out to do.

 "The law and the prophets" is Matthew's favorite expression for describing the whole of the Old Testament (see 5:17; 7:12; 11:13; 22:40). For Matthew, Jesus does not come to abolish but to fulfill both the Law and the Prophets. This two-part division contrasts somewhat with Luke's threefold reference to the Law, the Prophets, and the Psalms (see Luke 24:44).

This interpretation sheds an interesting light on Jesus' claims in Matthew 5:17-18. Jesus says that not even the smallest part of Mosaic Law will cease to have full authority over the lives of God's people "until heaven and earth pass away." It was a common feature of Jewish eschatology (the Jewish understanding of the "end times") around the time of Jesus that the coming of a new heaven and a new earth would be inaugurated by the resurrection of the righteous dead. Matthew and Paul both saw in Jesus' death a fulfillment of the law that not only brought it to completion, but superseded it when Jesus rose from the dead. The heaven and the earth as they knew them had passed away; a new heaven and a new earth have begun in Christ's resurrection and will be completed with our own resurrections.

Matthew, more than any other gospel, stresses that the deeds and words of Jesus are a fulfillment of the Old Testament. The law given to and for Israel is fulfilled by the life and death of Jesus, who is completely faithful to God. With the rising of Christ from the dead there is a new teaching given to the whole world by which righteousness is to flourish: the Good News of Jesus Christ. Indeed, after the resurrection, when Jesus commissions the apostles to make disciples of all nations, no mention is made of the law. It is the Gospel they are to preach:

> Then Jesus approached and said to them, "All power in heaven and on earth has been given to me. Go, therefore, and make disciples of all nations, baptizing them in the name of the Father, and of the Son, and of the holy Spirit, teaching them to observe all that I have commanded you. And behold, I am with you always, until the end of the age." (Matt 28:18-20)

THE ANTITHESES

In Matthew 5:21-48, we encounter six of Jesus' instructions for living righteously. Each of these teachings offers within itself a sharp contrast with what appears to be commonly accepted religious ethics and customs of the times. The way Jesus contrasts his teachings with accepted practice is quite profound. As we will see at the end of the Sermon on the Mount, the crowds will react to his teachings with astonishment because he teaches with such authority (7:28-29). Nowhere is his authoritative teaching style more evident than in these six passages. Here Jesus reinterprets familiar religious and ethical sayings that come from the Torah (the law of Moses contained in the Pentateuch). Jesus begins each of these teachings by saying "You have heard . . ." and then quotes a certain axiom or tenet of the law. He then offers a new teaching based solely on his own authority, beginning with the phrase "But I say to you . . ." Scholars often refer to these instructions as "the antitheses" (or opposites) because of the sharp contrast between the familiar teaching and Jesus' new teaching.

Some scholars contend that Jesus was doing no more than interpreting the true intent of Mosaic Law in authentic rabbinical style, and in making this argument, they present a great deal of evidence from numerous rabbis. The words of many of those rabbis, however, first appear in writings long after Jesus' time. Some noted scholars such as John P. Meier assert that

Jesus sometimes intends to teach the true intent of Mosaic Law and, at least occasionally, deliberately overrules it. However, Jesus certainly regards what is written in the Torah as the word of God, as is evident in his responses to Satan while being tempted (Matt 4:1-11). As we proceed, wherever possible, it will be shown that when Jesus changes the understanding of a commandment or a precept, while he may demand more or something other than the commandment originally stated, he is not denying the fundamental validity of the commandment.

In the antitheses, Matthew is communicating that these teachings are universal; they aren't just part of a higher ethic communicated to his disciples. In saying, "You have heard that it was said to your ancestors," everyone in the crowd recognizes that Jesus is referring to the law delivered to all of Israel while they were assembled around Moses at Mount Sinai, just as they themselves are gathered at a mount at the feet of Jesus. What Jesus asserts in these six "antitheses" he intends as authoritative teaching for all who hear them.

Jesus teaches from a position of **authority,** though not an authority that was universally recognized at the time. He pronounces well-accepted beliefs of Jewish tradition and then proclaims "but *I* say to you . . ." or "Amen, *I* say to you" (5:21-48; emphasis added). Jesus also claims the authority to forgive sins (e.g., 9:1-8) and heals at times that seem to disregard strictly held Sabbath laws (e.g., 12:9-14). By the time Jesus arrives in Jerusalem, the Jewish leaders question his right to speak and act with such authority (21:23). These leaders claim authority by virtue of their religious and social roles. But throughout the Gospel of Matthew, Jesus demonstrates that his authority comes directly from an intimate relationship with his Father, the author (the true "*author*ity") of all that exists (see 11:27).

Teaching about Anger

²¹"You have heard that it was said to your ancestors, 'You shall not kill; and whoever kills will be liable to judgment.' ²²But I say to you, whoever is angry with his brother will be liable to judgment, and whoever says to his brother, 'Raqa,' will be answerable to the Sanhedrin, and whoever says, 'You fool,' will be liable to fiery Gehenna. ²³Therefore, if you bring your gift to the altar, and there recall that your brother has anything against you, ²⁴leave your gift there at the altar, go first and be reconciled with your brother, and then come and offer your gift. ²⁵Settle with your opponent quickly while on the way to court with him. Otherwise your opponent will hand you over to the judge, and the judge will hand you over to the guard, and you will be thrown into prison. ²⁶Amen, I say to you, you will not be released until you have paid the last penny.

continue

Teaching about Anger (5:21-26)

Everyone gets angry sometimes, even Jesus! In Mark 3:1-5 Jesus is in a synagogue on the Sabbath when he encounters a man with a withered hand. When Jesus notices that some Pharisees are watching him closely, hoping he will heal the man on the Sabbath so that they can accuse him of breaking the third commandment against working on the Sabbath, he responds with anger:

> He said to the man with the withered hand, "Come up here before us." Then he said to them, "Is it lawful to do good on the sabbath rather than to do evil, to save life rather than to destroy it?" But they remained silent. Looking around at them with anger and grieved at their hardness of heart, he said to the man, "Stretch out your hand." He stretched it out and his hand was restored. (Mark 3:3-5)

We find another example of Jesus' anger in his response to the buying and selling that took place in the temple area:

Jesus entered the temple area and drove out all those engaged in selling and buying there. He overturned the tables of the money changers and the seats of those who were selling doves. And he said to them, "It is written: / 'My house shall be a house of prayer,' / but you are making it a den of thieves." (Matt 21:12-13)

When Jesus condemns anger, he does so in the context of the commandment against killing. Jesus knows that unchecked anger motivates murder. While Paul was no stranger to anger himself (he goes so far as to call the Galatian Christians "stupid" in his anger with them; Gal 3:1), he also recognizes the danger of anger and warns that we must quickly let go of it: "Be angry but do not sin; do not let the sun set on your anger" (Eph 4:26).

In addition to condemning anger, Jesus warns of severe punishment for those who assail others with words of contempt ("raqa" can be translated as "blockhead," "dolt," or something equally contemptuous). Calling someone a fool can easily spring from anger, but there is something more here than just the condemnation of anger. In a culture like ancient Israel's where public honor (having a good reputation) was absolutely critical, public insults could be attempts to shame someone, thus killing a person's public standing. Today, even insults delivered in private are often mean-spirited attempts to kill another person's honor or sense of self-worth. They can be intentional efforts to murder the soul of a person.

In Matthew 5:22, Jesus warns of the severe judgment that awaits those who express contempt for others—either temporal by way of the Sanhedrin or after death in Gehenna (to be discussed later). In 5:23-24, he goes even further by warning that our worship of God has no value if we have offended someone without seeking reconciliation with him or her. Jesus says that if we approach the altar with a gift (as an act of worship) and remember that we have given offense to someone, seeking forgiveness from the one we have offended must come before we offer our gift to God. As difficult as it might be to seek forgiveness, it is also an opportunity for the one offended to offer forgiveness, allowing both parties to participate in God's forgiving nature.

Teaching about Adultery (5:27-30)

"You shall not commit adultery" is the sixth of the Ten Commandments written on the stone tablets God gave Moses on Mount Sinai. It must have sounded like an incredible understatement to hear Jesus say, "You have heard that it was said." Given the moral gravity of the Ten Commandments and the prominence given to them in all of Old Testament Scripture, the commandment would be something that rang with constancy in the ears of the crowd. This would make it all the more shocking to hear Jesus, no matter how highly regarded as a teacher and a wonder worker, extend the range of the commandment with a declaration from his own claim to authority.

Jesus, however, is in no way about to undo the commandment. Rather, what Jesus says next expands the parameter of the covenant, forbidding not just the physical act of adultery but also the harboring of lust in the heart that both tempts and leads to adultery. Just as anger and insults are the prelude to violence and murder, lust can lead to adultery.

Those prone to scrupulosity might see in Jesus' teaching a reason for condemning themselves for feeling attraction to someone to whom they aren't married, but that is far from what is intended. Jesus warns against the kind of lust (not simple attraction) that willfully engages in fantasizing about the act of adultery, indulging in the heart what adultery accomplishes in the physical act.

Adultery is such a serious sin that Jesus goes on to warn that it must be avoided at all costs. He paints an extremely vivid picture of the lengths one ought to go to avoid it or any sin: plucking out one's eye if that is the cause for sin or cutting off one's right hand if that is the cause. Of course, it is never the hand or the eye that actually causes one to sin. It is the heart that desires what is forbidden; it is the will that commits one to sin. Changing one's heart and reforming one's will requires an ef-

Teaching about Adultery

27"You have heard that it was said, 'You shall not commit adultery.' 28But I say to you, everyone who looks at a woman with lust has already committed adultery with her in his heart. 29If your right eye causes you to sin, tear it out and throw it away. It is better for you to lose one of your members than to have your whole body thrown into Gehenna. 30And if your right hand causes you to sin, cut it off and throw it away. It is better for you to lose one of your members than to have your whole body go into Gehenna.

continue

fort far different from physical dismemberment, but Jesus' deliberate exaggeration is meant to bring home the seriousness with which the endeavor to have a pure heart should be undertaken.

The fiery imagery of Gehenna in verse 29 is meant to be startling. It refers metaphorically to the valley of Hinnom, located southwest of Jerusalem. Called "Ben-hinnom" in Jeremiah, it was where worshipers of Moloch offered their children to their idol in a fiery holocaust (Jer 7:31). By the time of Jesus' ministry, Gehenna symbolized the place of fiery torment where the enemies of God would be consigned after death. Because its use is metaphorical, it cannot be understood in an absolutely literal sense, but it is clearly meant to issue a stark warning that anything that leads one to sin must be removed from one's life.

Teaching about Divorce (5:31-32)

In Deuteronomy 24:1, Mosaic Law acknowledges that a husband may divorce his wife after becoming "displeased with her because he finds in her something indecent" by providing her with a written "bill of divorce." In Matthew 19:8, Jesus tells the Pharisees that Moses allowed this practice "[b]ecause of the hardness of your hearts." Mark's gospel also reports that Jesus forbade divorce. There Jesus

---

Teaching about Divorce

³¹"It was also said, 'Whoever divorces his wife must give her a bill of divorce.' ³²But I say to you, whoever divorces his wife (unless the marriage is unlawful) causes her to commit adultery, and whoever marries a divorced woman commits adultery.

continue

---

tells the Pharisees that the permanence of marriage is revealed in the Genesis 2:19-24 account of creation, saying:

> "But from the beginning of creation, 'God made them male and female. For this reason a man shall leave his father and mother [and be joined to his wife], and the two shall become one flesh.' So they are no longer two but one flesh. Therefore what God has joined together, no human being must separate." (Mark 10:6-9)

In the Markan account, there is no qualification permitting divorce, whereas in Matthew we read what has come to be known as the "exception clause" (placed in parentheses in our translation): "unless the marriage is unlawful." The Greek word that is translated into English here as "unlawful" is *porneia* (from which our word "pornography" is derived), but the meaning of *porneia* in Matthew's context has been widely debated. Many Catholic biblical scholars believe the exception created by *porneia* was a clarification made from within Matthew's church community (which began as an almost entirely Jewish congregation) when confronted by the fact that some Gentile converts came into the church with spousal relationships that were considered incestuous by Jews. Incest is therefore one possible meaning or intention of *porneia* in this context. We know that Paul had to deal with incest within the Corinthian church (1 Cor 5:1-2). If incest is the intended exception in Matthew 5:32, then Matthew's community likely required divorce

in circumstances where the relationship was deemed incestuous. They probably considered the marriage invalid from the beginning.

Was Jesus using his divine authority to change Mosaic Law, which had always been considered to be divine revelation? Or was he only interpreting the true intent of Mosaic Law and therefore only using his authority to set the record straight? There seems to be no end to this debate. Those who think Jesus actually changed Mosaic Law stress the fact that Deuteronomy 24:1 acknowledges the practice of a man divorcing his wife, which Jesus seems to be overturning. On the other side of the debate are several factors. One is that Jesus states his position on the basis of what is found in Genesis 2, which is also part of the Torah and which he says reveals God's true intent in giving the law. The prophet Malachi also reveals God's hatred of divorce:

> [T]he Lord no longer takes note of your offering
>   or accepts it favorably from your hand.
> And you say, "Why?"—
>   Because the Lord is witness
>   between you and the wife of your youth
> With whom you have broken faith,
>   though she is your companion, your
>   covenanted wife.
> Did he not make them one, with flesh and
>   spirit?
>   And what does the One require? Godly
>   offspring!
> You should be on guard, then, for your life,
>   and do not break faith with the wife of your
>   youth.
> For I hate divorce,
>   says the Lord, the God of Israel.
>   (Mal 2:13b-16a)

It is important to note that what Jesus says about divorce has produced far more than just scholarly debate. Divorce and remarriage within the Catholic Church is a matter that has caused great anguish in numerous families and has led many bishops and priests to seek truly pastoral means of caring for broken and blended families. In doing so, they acknowledge the tension between the authority of

Jesus' words and the significant challenges faced by many families today.

Teaching about Oaths (5:33-37)

The question that almost always surfaces following a study of Jesus' teaching about oaths is whether or not Jesus meant his words to be strictly observed as a commandment that superseded Mosaic Law (which severely punished making false oaths), or if Jesus simply wanted to put an end to idle or frivolous oaths.

A great deal of Mosaic Law involves the enforcement of oaths, no matter how lightly taken. No one who took an oath could later be freed from whatever they had bound themselves by an oath to do: "When a man makes a vow to the Lord or binds himself under oath to a pledge, he shall not violate his word, but must fulfill exactly the promise he has uttered" (Num 30:3). Women were similarly bound unless they lived in the house of their father, and he opposed her oath on the same day that he first learned of it (Num 30:4-6).

There was a time when making a solemn oath in the name of God brought with it the moral certainty that God would judge the person who swore to be truthful but nevertheless lied, even if the lie was never found out. The second commandment as found in Exodus 20:7 is clear: "You shall not invoke the name of the Lord, your God, *in vain*. For the Lord *will not leave unpunished* anyone who invokes his name *in vain*" (emphasis mine). However, by the time Jesus delivered the Sermon on the Mount, it appears that oath-taking carefully avoided using the name of God altogether.

In this antithesis, Jesus is very clear about oath-taking in general: do not swear at all (5:34a). Many of us think of "swearing" as the use of foul words or the use of titles of divinity in an irreverent matter. But originally "swearing" meant oath-taking. Legal testimony, for example, required the "swearing" of an oath (for example, "Do you swear to tell the truth, the whole truth, and nothing but the truth, so help you God?"). For centuries this teaching has proven to be a dilemma for many conscien-

Teaching about Oaths

[33]"Again you have heard that it was said to your ancestors, 'Do not take a false oath, but make good to the Lord all that you vow.' [34]But I say to you, do not swear at all; not by heaven, for it is God's throne; [35]nor by the earth, for it is his footstool; nor by Jerusalem, for it is the city of the great King. [36]Do not swear by your head, for you cannot make a single hair white or black. [37]Let your 'Yes' mean 'Yes,' and your 'No' mean 'No.' Anything more is from the evil one.

continue

tious Christians. Are we to refuse to take an oath in a court of law? Mennonites and others of the Anabaptist tradition firmly believe that Jesus meant to strictly forbid the taking of an oath under any circumstance. Catholic tradition has long suggested otherwise, that Christians can and must swear an oath when required by law to do so and that, in proper circumstances, governments can rightfully require the taking of oaths.

The Anabaptists give us a very important insight concerning Jesus' instructions concerning oath-taking, however. Their refusal to provide oaths to assure the truthfulness of their speech in any matter is rooted in something deeper than just the commandment aspect of Matthew 5:33-37. It is rooted in what Jesus says about anything we affirm or deny. We are always to tell the truth. Our "yes" is always to mean "yes," and our "no" is always to mean "no" (5:37). Even if we allow the possibility that Jesus wasn't delivering a new commandment but was simply preaching against the rampant ease with which his fellow Israelites would utter an oath, he was still teaching something very important to his disciples: be truthful in everything, and no one will ever need to require a sworn oath from you.

We know that leaders in the early church paid attention to Jesus' teaching about oaths because it is echoed in James 5:12: "But above

---

Teaching about Retaliation

³⁸"You have heard that it was said, 'An eye for an eye and a tooth for a tooth.' ³⁹But I say to you, offer no resistance to one who is evil. When someone strikes you on [your] right cheek, turn the other one to him as well. ⁴⁰If anyone wants to go to law with you over your tunic, hand him your cloak as well. ⁴¹Should anyone press you into service for one mile, go with him for two miles. ⁴²Give to the one who asks of you, and do not turn your back on one who wants to borrow.

continue

---

all, my brothers, do not swear, either by heaven or by earth or with any other oath, but let your 'Yes' mean 'Yes' and your 'No' mean 'No,' that you may not incur condemnation."

Teaching about Retaliation (5:38-42)

Mosaic Law clearly taught the basic law of retribution: "an eye for an eye, and a tooth for a tooth" (see Lev 24:19-20). Many biblical scholars tell us that "an eye for and eye and a tooth for a tooth" was originally intended as a restraint on the authority to punish. In other words, punishment could not exceed the violence of the criminal act itself. There is evidence, however, that the regulation came to be interpreted as mandatory sentencing: an eye *must* be taken for an eye; a tooth *must* be taken for a tooth. Jesus, while teaching that all the law must be observed, also taught with the authority to interpret the law according to its original intention. The *highest* command of the law was to embrace both justice and mercy. Later in Matthew, Jesus will quote Hosea 6:6 to the Pharisees: "Go and learn the meaning of the words, 'I desire mercy, not sacrifice' " (Matt 9:13).

Is Jesus complying with the original intention of the law when he tells his disciples to turn the other cheek if they have been slapped? He certainly is not contradicting the law, which we might assume in this context to *allow* a re-

turn of a slap for a slap ("an eye for an eye"). The law can be interpreted to mean the *most punishment allowable* is a slap for a slap, while Jesus is saying that *no punishment* is not only permissible under the law, but it is the correct recourse for his disciples.

Why is it desirable to turn the other cheek? Because the disciples' mission is to reveal God's mercy, not his justice. The offender knows that he deserves retaliation. But what an offender is most probably in greatest need of is an experience of God's mercy. In the Sermon on the Mount (and elsewhere in Matthew; see 24:9), disciples are to live and act in the name of Jesus. Whoever encounters them should see in them what they would expect from Jesus, for they are acting in his name. Non-retaliation on the part of the disciples is not simply an ethic of pacifism. It is to be interpreted as a sign of God's mercy, which is part of the proclamation of the kingdom of heaven.

Did Jesus' emphasis on mercy also lead him to teach pacifism? Pacifists are those who refuse to respond to violence with violence. Pacifists will defend themselves and their loved ones, just not violently. A true pacifist might well lose his or her life in an attempt to prevent violence being done to a loved one or innocent bystanders. Above all, pacifists believe in the sanctity of all life, especially human life. We know that Jesus Christ allowed himself to be crucified. Matthew and John are most explicit about Jesus rejecting the opportunity to resist his arrest:

> And behold, one of those who accompanied Jesus put his hand to his sword, drew it, and struck the high priest's servant, cutting off his ear. Then Jesus said to him, "Put your sword back into its sheath, for all who take the sword will perish by the sword. Do you think that I cannot call upon my Father and he will not provide me at this moment with more than twelve legions of angels?" (Matt 26:51-53)

> "This is why the Father loves me, because I lay down my life in order to take it up again. No one takes it from me, but I lay it down on my own. I have power to lay it down, and power to take it up again. This command I

have received from my Father." (John 10:17-18)

Taking all the evidence from his life and death, it is safe to say that if Jesus wasn't an ideological pacifist, he lived and died as a practicing one. But what did he call his disciples to be? Are Christians morally obliged to live by pacifist ideals? Early Christians were known for refusing military service, but that practice ended when the Roman Empire legalized and then later embraced Christianity as its official religion. For many centuries, the Catholic Church has taught the right to lethal self-defense and even the obligation of citizens to carry and use arms for the defense of their nation. More recently, however, the church has acknowledged the right of individual Catholics to be conscientious objectors. In other words, while lethal self-defense and national defense are morally permissible, pacifism can be embraced in good conscience as a Christian ethic.

Given this background, we still might ask whether these teachings of Jesus on non-retaliation are in conflict with self-defense and military service. Perhaps a closer look at the context of the Sermon on the Mount will shed light on this apparent dilemma. While the crowds are listening to Jesus with amazement, Jesus is personally instructing his disciples. They are the ones he is sending out to the "lost sheep of the house of Israel" to announce the good news of the kingdom of heaven (Matt 10:5-15). In committing themselves to that mission, it is essential that they embrace Jesus' teachings against retaliation. Just as he will die on the cross in order to be the ultimate expression of God's mercy and forgiveness, they too must be signs of mercy. They are to leave any judgment on those who reject or revile them to God:

> "As you enter a house, wish it peace. If the house is worthy, let your peace come upon it; if not, let your peace return to you. Whoever will not receive you or listen to your words— go outside that house or town and shake the dust from your feet. Amen, I say to you, it will be more tolerable for the land of Sodom and

Love of Enemies

43"You have heard that it was said, 'You shall love your neighbor and hate your enemy.' 44But I say to you, love your enemies, and pray for those who persecute you, 45that you may be children of your heavenly Father, for he makes his sun rise on the bad and the good, and causes rain to fall on the just and the unjust. 46For if you love those who love you, what recompense will you have? Do not the tax collectors do the same? 47And if you greet your brothers only, what is unusual about that? Do not the pagans do the same? 48So be perfect, just as your heavenly Father is perfect.

Gomorrah on the day of judgment than for that town." (Matt 10:12-15)

It may be that whether or not Jesus calls all Christians to embrace a specifically Christian form of pacifism is a matter left to individual conscience and depends upon one's particular circumstances. But one thing is clear: in all circumstances, we are to strive to be like Jesus, who always chose to turn the other cheek, walk the extra mile, and never turned his back on anyone who needed him.

Love of Enemies (5:43-48)

In the Old Testament the Israelites are explicitly told to love their neighbor (Lev 19:18). Nowhere in the Old Testament are they told to hate their enemy. In this specific instance, when Jesus says "You have heard that it was said," we have no record of any religious authority ever expressing that as a teaching. But of course in Jesus' time, Israel was an oral culture. For the common person, almost all religious instruction and belief was handed on by the spoken word. For all we know, the saying that "you shall love your neighbor and hate your enemy" may have been a popular saying of the day.

The book of Genesis reveals that humans are created in God's image (Gen 1:26). By calling Jesus "God with us," Matthew doubles down on humanity as the image of God. Jesus is actually God in our midst, as one of us. Then, in providing us with Jesus' teachings in the Sermon on the Mount, Matthew gives us the highest ideals of Christianity concerning how we are to respect and love everyone—including our enemies—for everyone is created in the image of God.

Particular attention should be paid to the phrase "that you may be children of your heavenly Father, for he makes his sun rise on the bad and the good" (5:45). God is Father to all, the good and the bad. The fact that there are bad people and that they might be our enemies is not dismissed. What the phrase implies, however, is that we are all—whether good or bad, ally or enemy—family. We are to love our enemies because however alienated they may be from us, they are not alien to us. They are family, and to hate them is to fall into the sinful trap that snared Cain, who slew his brother Abel.

The difficulty in being told to love our enemies peaks, however, in what follows in Jesus' teaching. We are to love our enemies because God cares for both the just and the unjust. And because God is our heavenly Father, we are expected to be perfect, just as our Father is perfect. How can we be as perfect as God? Luke also hands on this teaching concerning loving our enemies, but in Luke's account, Jesus tells his disciples to "be merciful, just as [also] your Father is merciful" (Luke 6:36). When speaking of the Father's love for all of us, just or unjust, there is no contradiction, no antithesis, between being perfect and being merciful. Matthew's Greek word for "perfect" could also be translated as "whole" in the sense that we become whole when we become all that we were intended to be. "Perfect" can seem to us to be something hard and inflexible, a frozen ideal. Being whole, though, is something we all want to be. It will take mercy to get there.

EXPLORING LESSON TWO

1. a) Salt both preserves food and enhances its flavor. Who has given you a fresh or an enhanced appreciation for the Good News (5:13)?

   Women's Bible Study
   Fr Toup's Rejoice Series
   Dynamic Cath. — Best Lent/Advent series

   b) Who would you identify as the brightest lights in your world (5:14-15)? What makes them shine so brightly?

   Bishop Barron
   Pope Francis

2. What are two different ways to understand what Jesus meant by saying he came to fulfill the law (5:17-18)? (See Eph 2:13-15.)

   — He came as the new Adam & brought forth the new earth & new heaven.

   — For Gentiles — He replaced the law of Moses with a new faith in One God — Heavenly Father.

3. How has the experience of giving or receiving an apology made a difference for you in a personal relationship (5:21-26)?

   Made right relationship w/ my Mom.

4. What authority does Jesus cite in extending the parameters of the commandments, as in the sixth commandment (5:27-28)? (See 7:28-29; Deut 5:18.)

   "He taught w/ Authority (God) not as the Scribes"

5. Concerning Jesus' teaching on divorce, what is probably meant by the phrase "unless the marriage is unlawful" (5:32)? Why is that phrase usually found in parentheses?

Incestous — which was common w/ the Corinthian Church.

6. What purpose do oaths serve in our society? Why would Jesus caution against taking oaths (5:33-37)?

Swearing to tell the truth; Swearing to uphold laws of the country & Constitution. Because an oath is to be upheld —

7. a) What different positions have Christians taken in regard to when and how to keep Jesus' teaching on self-defense and love of enemies (5:38-48)?

Conscientious objector in times of war, OR — signing up to defend the US

b) In what ways does this teaching challenge you? How do you (or how can you) pray about it?

I pray for world peace.

8. Who are some figures (famous or otherwise) who contemplated Matthew 5:38-48 and became conscientious objectors or embraced nonviolent civil disobedience?

Muhammad Ali
Dave Barry

Barriga Bros.
Gandhi

CLOSING PRAYER

Prayer

"Love your enemies, and pray for those who persecute you, that you may be children of your heavenly Father . . ." (Matt 5:44-45)

Your life, Jesus, teaches the power of love poured out in forgiveness and reconciliation. Place a desire in our hearts, and the opportunities needed, to make amends with others—those we have offended and those who have been hurtful to us. We pray now to accept the grace you offer. We pray for those in need of this grace, especially . . .

LESSON THREE

Matthew 6:1-21

Begin your personal study and group discussion with a simple and sincere prayer such as:

Prayer

Jesus, you teach us to listen to your words and imitate your deeds. Be with me now as I listen for your voice, and help me to become more like you.

Read the Bible text of Matthew 6:1-21 found in the outside columns of pages 47–56, highlighting what stands out to you.

Read the accompanying commentary to add to your understanding.

Respond to the questions on pages 58–60, Exploring Lesson Three.

The Closing Prayer on page 60 is for your personal use and may be used at the end of group discussion.

6:1-21 OUR FATHER, WHO SEES IN SECRET

Matthew 6 begins with warnings and instructions from Jesus concerning pious behaviors, that is, religious practices that could be undertaken for egocentric or prideful reasons. Cultural anthropologists describe Israel and much of the Mediterranean world of Jesus' time as an honor-shame society. Honor-shame societies are those in which one's public reputation is of extreme importance. In Israel at that time, this was not just a matter of one's personal reputation, but of a shared sense of honor or shame that was affixed to one's wider family, or even village, clan, or tribe. In honor-shame societies there is no in-between; interaction with others is always undertaken with either an aura of honor or of shame, and one's reputation is always either built up or torn down.

Jesus warns the crowds, and his disciples in particular, that the only reward given for "righteous deeds" that are performed in public in order to gain public approval or honor will be the recognition the public gives them. Jesus is clear that although public honor is greatly valued in human society, it is not the way God rewards the righteous.

Truly righteous deeds, in the context of Matthew 6:1-21, are not deeds performed for the sake of being praised by others or even for the sake of earning one's salvation. Rather, they are the fruit blossoming from those who are already living in covenant relationship with the God who saves. When righteous deeds are performed for the purpose of demonstrating to others that one has gained a special relationship with God, they undermine that relationship. They have ceased to be that life-giving fruit borne of a relationship with God.

Jesus does, however, imply that there is a "recompense" from the heavenly Father for those who perform righteous deeds quietly or in secret. This might cause some to think that Jesus didn't go far enough in teaching proper motivation for the performance of righteous deeds. Why still promise a reward for good deeds? Shouldn't doing the right thing be done

for its own sake? Would a truly good person need the promise of a divine reward to motivate his or her actions?

Elsewhere Matthew informs us of one of the chief rewards given to those who live according to Jesus' teachings. The reward is a special rest from life's heavy burdens:

> "Come to me, all you who labor and are burdened, and I will give you rest. Take my yoke upon you and learn from me, for I am meek and humble of heart; and you will find rest for yourselves. For my yoke is easy, and my burden light." (Matt 11:28-30)

If the proper performance of righteous deeds is to do them because they are expressions of our covenant relationship with God, then it should follow that the recompense for performing them is found in that very relationship. That is to say, God rewards truly righteous deeds by being present to us, even in gifting us with the ability and power to perform the deeds that flow out of our covenantal relationship with God.

Teaching about Almsgiving (6:1-4)

The English word "alms" is derived from a Greek word indicating a kindness or a merciful inclination. However, its use in deutero-canonical books (Old Testament books written in Greek closer to the time of Jesus) and the New Testament indicates a gift of charity to someone who is severely impoverished, that is, someone who cannot survive without charitable gifts being given to them.

Among many Jews of Jesus' day, giving alms was a sure sign that one was building up treasure with God. This concurs, for example, with the testimony Tobit gives to his son Tobiah:

> "Give alms from your possessions. Do not turn your face away from any of the poor, so that God's face will not be turned away from you. Give in proportion to what you own. If you have great wealth, give alms out of your abundance; if you have but little, do not be afraid to give alms even of that little. You will be storing up a goodly treasure for yourself against the day of adversity. For almsgiving delivers from death and keeps one from entering into Darkness. Almsgiving is a worthy offering in the sight of the Most High for all who practice it." (Tobit 4:7-11)

We find another example in Luke's gospel when Jesus encourages his disciples to be generous in almsgiving: "Sell your belongings and give alms. Provide money bags for yourselves that do not wear out, an inexhaustible treasure in heaven that no thief can reach nor moth destroy" (Luke 12:33).

In the book of Acts (10:1-49), the Gentile centurion Cornelius receives an angelic vision in which he learns that the apostle Peter is about to visit him. Cornelius is initially struck with fear, but the angel reassures him: "Your prayers and almsgiving have ascended as a memorial offering before God" (Acts 10:4).

In both the Old and New Testaments, almsgiving is a righteous deed. It builds up a treasure house with God when it is done as an act of God's love for the poor rather than as an act of one's own righteousness for public display. Jesus is clear that almsgiving ceases to be righteous when it becomes a means of buying a reputation for being righteous. The focus is entirely misdirected when the purpose of almsgiving becomes self-centered. The purpose of

CHAPTER 6

Teaching about Almsgiving

[1]"[But] take care not to perform righteous deeds in order that people may see them; otherwise, you will have no recompense from your heavenly Father. [2]When you give alms, do not blow a trumpet before you, as the hypocrites do in the synagogues and in the streets to win the praise of others. Amen, I say to you, they have received their reward. [3]But when you give alms, do not let your left hand know what your right is doing, [4]so that your almsgiving may be secret. And your Father who sees in secret will repay you.

Teaching about Prayer

[5]"When you pray, do not be like the hypocrites, who love to stand and pray in the synagogues and on street corners so that others may

continue

almsgiving is to help the poor, who bear the image of God, achieve some semblance of the dignity they deserve.

Many in modern society are wary of beggars and the homeless to the point of criticizing those who give them alms. The fear is that by attracting the presence of panhandlers, businesses suffer, crime rises (along with alcohol and drug abuse), and the possibility of gainful employment may be shirked for easier access to monetary gain. These fears are understandable, but they do not negate Scripture's consistent call to give to the poor. Today, there are a wide variety of ways to "give alms," including contributing to charitable agencies that are dedicated to helping the poor achieve lives that reflect their God-given dignity.

Teaching about Prayer (6:5-8)

Today, praying out loud in the public square, unless part of a gathering of like-minded believers, will give you a reputation, but not necessarily for being righteous! Some see them. Amen, I say to you, they have received their reward. ⁶But when you pray, go to your inner room, close the door, and pray to your Father in secret. And your Father who sees in secret will repay you. ⁷In praying, do not babble like the pagans, who think that they will be heard because of their many words. ⁸Do not be like them. Your Father knows what you need before you ask him.

continue

the learned you have revealed them to the childlike. Yes, Father, such has been your gracious will." (Luke 10:21; cf. Matt 11:25)

But often when Jesus prays, he seeks solitude. He withdraws from the crowds and even from his disciples and prays to his Father without being observed. After feeding the five thousand in Matthew 14:13-21 (which occurs following a previous attempt to go into a deserted place), Jesus resumes his plan to pray in seclusion: "he went up on the mountain by himself to pray. When it was evening he was there alone" (Matt 14:23).

In this teaching of Jesus, we also find the fertile seeds of contemplative prayer, especially in his exhortation to "go to your inner room, close the door, and pray to your Father in secret." To pray without words, using only the consistent effort to focus heart and mind on God's abiding presence in all things and beyond all things, is just a small step deeper within one's "inner room."

A criticism of many traditional prayer practices of Catholics and other Christians is that they violate Jesus' command in Matthew 6:7-8. For example, it is said that the repetition of the Hail Mary in the rosary (there are more than fifty in any one recitation of the rosary) ends up being "babbling"—a meaningless attempt to woo God's favor through a multiplication of words. The rosary itself is historically related to monastic prayer and the Liturgy of the Hours, in which the 150 psalms are eventually recited throughout the course of the liturgical year during set times of day. Many priests and religious admit that it can become a mind-numbing practice. But does that make praying the Liturgy of the Hours—or any other repetitive prayer—"babbling"?

The translation of this passage in the New Revised Standard Version may help bring greater clarity in this matter. It says: "do not heap up empty phrases as the Gentiles do" (Matt 6:7). Jesus is not primarily warning his disciples against repetition or long prayers but against using words—any words—as an attempt win God's favor simply because one has

would call the one praying a nuisance; others might use the term "nut case." I have often wondered if Jesus' criticism applies to those saying grace in a restaurant, whether praying quietly by oneself or aloud at a table of friends and family. Motivation and circumstances for public prayer seem necessary for discernment.

In these verses of the sermon, Jesus is criticizing hypocrites whose public prayer is meant not to bring them into the presence of God, but rather to call attention to themselves. There are times and places for public prayer, but sensitivity to the purpose of the prayer is paramount. To be sure, praying aloud together is a commandment:

You shall rejoice in the presence of the LORD, your God, with your sons and daughters, your male and female slaves, as well as with the Levite within your gates, who has no hereditary portion with you. (Deut 12:12)

Jesus' own life and teachings bear witness to the importance of outward prayer. Jesus loudly praised God in the presence of his disciples. For example, in Luke's gospel, when his disciples return to him after a successful mission of proclaiming the Good News of the kingdom, Jesus seems unable to restrain his joy:

At that very moment he rejoiced [in] the holy Spirit and said, "I give you praise, Father, Lord of heaven and earth, for although you have hidden these things from the wise and employed vocal sounds for long enough to get God's attention. In other words, prayer is not a barter system in which words alone are sufficient coinage to buy what one asks for.

The words we speak in prayer can be significant, heartfelt, and meaningful. They can also be extremely familiar, such as the Our Father and the Hail Mary, or even the many psalms repeated over and over again in the Liturgy of the Hours. It is true that the familiarity of these prayers can sometimes disengage our minds from their content—but that does not necessarily make them "babbling." As long as our desire to pray is sincere, our words reach out to God. In this way they achieve what Jesus himself acknowledges is our desire in prayer: to "be heard." This assurance that God hears our prayers can remove the temptation to babble on for the sake of multiplying words. Sometimes the most profound prayer happens when we compose our souls in silence in God's presence.

Jesus' warning about "babbling" is only a part of his teachings on prayer. To learn what it means to be heard by God, we also need to know what it is we are seeking from God when we pray. This is what Jesus will teach us in the Lord's Prayer. The Father knows what we need before we ask, so what we are seeking most when we pray is not what we want, but what God wills.

The Lord's Prayer (6:9-15)

Both the Gospel of Matthew and the Gospel of Luke include versions of what we now call the Lord's Prayer or the Our Father (see Luke 11:2-4). Of course, here in Matthew's gospel the prayer is part of a sermon. When Jesus teaches the prayer to his disciples in Luke's gospel, it is because his disciples have seen him praying and ask to learn how to pray: "He was praying in a certain place, and when he had finished, one of his disciples said to him, 'Lord, teach us to pray just as John taught his disciples'" (Luke 11:1).

Matthew's version of the Our Father has more content than Luke's and is closest to the version of the Our Father that many of us

---

The Lord's Prayer

⁹"This is how you are to pray:

Our Father in heaven,
  hallowed be your name,
  ¹⁰your kingdom come,
your will be done,
  on earth as in heaven.
¹¹Give us today our daily bread;
¹²and forgive us our debts,
  as we forgive our debtors;ᶠ
¹³and do not subject us to the final test,
  but deliver us from the evil one.

¹⁴If you forgive others their transgressions, your heavenly Father will forgive you. ¹⁵But if you do not forgive others, neither will your Father forgive your transgressions.

continue

---

memorized as children. Certainly one perennial question surrounding the Our Father is whether Jesus intended it to be memorized and repeated by rote or, as is more likely, whether he intended it to be the basis for all our prayer. In that case it would be more like a list of categories for prayerful attention and not simply a final set of words we are to employ in prayer. That is not to say that repeating the Lord's Prayer word for word is wrong. What it does suggest is that when we pray with other words, we should ask ourselves if our prayer embraces what the Our Father teaches about prayer.

Our Father. The first difference to note between Matthew's version of the Lord's Prayer and Luke's is that God is addressed in Matthew as "Our Father" and in Luke simply as "Father." This does not mean that Luke's version was intended to communicate a more individualistic relationship between the one praying and God, but Matthew's version avoids the possibility of giving that impression. The confidence with which we are to address God as "Father" is astounding enough, but, in addressing God as "Our Father," we cannot avoid the communal nature of the prayer. All who pray it are, in fact, proclaiming that they are brothers and sisters to one another.

God is called "Father" of ancient Israel a number of times in the Old Testament. In Isaiah 63:15-16, a heartfelt plea is made to God, begging that he remember Israel's relationship to God as one of father and child:

> Look down from heaven and regard us
>   from your holy and glorious palace!
> Where is your zealous care and your might,
>   your surge of pity?
> Your mercy hold not back!
>   For you are our father.
> Were Abraham not to know us,
>   nor Israel to acknowledge us,
> You, LORD, are our father,
>   our redeemer you are named from of old.

In Hosea, God proclaims himself Israel's father: "When Israel was a child I loved him, / out of Egypt I called my son" (11:1). (This verse is quoted in Matthew 2:15 when Joseph brings Jesus and Mary back to Israel from Egypt.) Since the fatherhood of God is something attested to in the Old Testament, it is not something that was first revealed by Jesus. In the Old Testament, however, it was far more common for Israelites to address or describe God as the God of their fathers Abraham, Isaac, and Jacob (Gen 32:10; Exod 3:6). The consistency and intimacy with which Jesus invokes God as his father is unique to the New Testament.

In the late 1960s Joachim Jeremias claimed that Jesus' use of "Abba" was the Aramaic equivalent of a child referring to his father as "Daddy." This continues to be a popular assertion with preachers, but scholars today find little evidence for the claim. What is far more certain is that calling God his Father did suggest an intimacy with the Creator, one that eventually led simple Christians, theologians, and church authorities to regard Jesus as the Son of God in an absolutely unique way. It eventually became a settled matter of faith that

Jesus of Nazareth was the incarnation of the eternally preexistent Word (John 1:1)—not just *a son of God*, but *God the Son*.

When Christianity arose from the Gospel proclaimed by Jesus' followers, Christians came to understand that faith in Christ had given them a share in the intimate relationship between Jesus and the Father. All the titles and appellations showered on the Most High from ancient Israel could not compete with Jesus' assurance that God is our loving Father. This understanding became central to Paul's proclamation of the Gospel, even to the point of making it the definitive proof of the gift of the Spirit in the lives of the baptized:

> As proof that you are children, God sent the spirit of his Son into our hearts, crying out, "Abba, Father!" (Gal 4:6)

> For you did not receive a spirit of slavery to fall back into fear, but you received a spirit of adoption, through which we cry, *"Abba, Father!"* The Spirit itself bears witness with our spirit that we are children of God, and if children, then heirs, heirs of God and joint heirs with Christ, if only we suffer with him so that we may also be glorified with him. (Rom 8:15-17)

In heaven. Throughout biblical times, heaven was conceived of as a literal place up above the sky. Actually, there were thought to be three heavens. The first was simply the sky itself, often translated as "firmament" or as "dome," which was the realm of the sun in the day and was filled with stars and the moon at night. The firmament was a physical barrier separating the waters above the sky from the waters of the sea and the waters beneath the earth. Above the firmament was a second heaven, which contained the waters that shed the rains that fell on earth. Above that was the third heaven, which was the realm of God and the heavenly court. Paul references this third heaven in this interesting account about himself, written to the Corinthians:

> I know someone in Christ who, fourteen years ago (whether in the body or out of the body I

do not know, God knows), was caught up to the third heaven. And I know that this person (whether in the body or out of the body I do not know, God knows) was caught up into Paradise and heard ineffable things, which no one may utter. (2 Cor 12:2-4)

We no longer think of heaven, the heaven that is the realm of God, as a physical location in the scientifically knowable universe. But "our Father in heaven" is the simplest, most traditional way of referring to God's transcendence. God is everywhere, including here on earth, but here we are free to ignore God's presence and to frustrate God's purposes in many ways. So in praying to "our Father in heaven," we are seeking to present ourselves to God in all of God's transcendence—beyond any mess we as humans have made here on earth and past the blinders we place on God's presence in our midst.

Hallowed be your name. The first and second commandments remind us of our obligation to have high regard for God's holiness (Deut 5:6-11). New Testament scholars see a different emphasis in the Lord's Prayer. In teaching this prayer, Jesus is mindful of having commissioned the disciples to continue his own mission of proclaiming the nearness (the "at-handedness") of the kingdom of heaven, which the Lord's Prayer makes explicit in the very next verse (6:10). In praying as Jesus taught us, we are not just telling God that we acknowledge his holiness, but we are asking God to make his kingdom manifest by causing the name of God to be hallowed throughout the earth.

Your kingdom come. If you ask Christians what their ultimate hope is, most will probably say "to go to heaven." Surprisingly then, in this prayer Jesus taught his disciples, the one most central to Christian faith, there is no mention of the Christian hope of going to heaven. Instead, there is a plea for God's kingdom to arrive on earth. The prayer continues with the key to bringing this about.

Your will be done, on earth as in heaven. What are we praying for when we pray for God's will to be done? Through the prophet Micah, Israel was given the simplest of instructions for discerning and performing the will of God: "You have been told, O mortal, what is good, / and what the LORD requires of you: / Only to do justice and to love goodness, / and to walk humbly with your God" (6:8). And in identifying the two greatest commandments, Jesus gave us nearly the same instructions in commandments taken directly from the law of Moses:

> "You shall love the Lord, your God, with all your heart, with all your soul, and with all your mind [Deut 6:5]. This is the greatest and the first commandment. The second is like it: You shall love your neighbor as yourself [Lev 19:18]. The whole law and the prophets depend on these two commandments." (Matt 22:37-40)

Thus it seems that in praying for God's will to be done on earth as in heaven, we are praying for harmony among human beings and between human beings and God. Of course, when it comes to discerning exactly what this means in each of our lives, the situation becomes a little more complicated. Each one of us possesses a unique set of gifts and a unique set of challenges. Discerning the will of God in the context of our particular gifts and challenges requires time spent in prayer and perhaps even the skilled insights of a spiritual director. Jesus sent his disciples out into the world to proclaim the nearness of the kingdom of heaven and to continue the healing, transforming works of his ministry. In answering this call, we each find our own ways of participating in God's will on earth.

Give us today our daily bread. What is our daily bread? It is unclear what exactly is meant by the customary translation "daily." Some early translations interpreted it as "needful bread" and still others as a "bread of the future." It would seem a bit strange, though, to ask to receive today the bread we will need tomorrow. When God provided manna in the wilderness (Exod 16), the Israelites were only given enough for one day, except on the day before the Sabbath, when they would gather enough for the day of rest ahead. But could "bread of the future" be referring to the eschatological bread—the bread we will dine on in the kingdom of heaven?

The difficulty in providing a definitive translation arises from the uniqueness of the Greek word *epiousios* (the word translated here as "daily"). It is a word that never appeared in any known Greek writings before its appearance in both Matthew's (6:11) and Luke's (11:3) versions of the Lord's Prayer. It appears nowhere else in the New Testament. (Whenever "daily" appears elsewhere in the New Testament, the Greek word is *hemera*, not *epiousios*.)

Because the Greek preposition *epi* is used frequently to imply greatness or superiority, and because *ousios* appears related to the word for substance, Jerome once translated *epiousios* with a Latin word that means "super-substantial." More and more Catholic scholars are affirming that the original sense of the word should be translated into English as "supernatural." If this is the original meaning, it suggests that this is no ordinary bread that we are asking to receive on a daily basis. Many, including the formidable New Testament scholar Eugene LaVerdiere, assert that it is a reference to the Eucharist.

Many years ago, one of my English literature professors informed our class that one of the hallmarks of the Jesuit poet Gerard Manley Hopkins' work was his effective use of "deliberate ambiguity." My professor explained that Hopkins employed words and let them have more than one meaning. He warned that we would miss what Hopkins was conveying in his poetry if we insisted on a single definition. We were to read his poetry with our minds open to more than one perception of his meaning, which made Hopkins worth reading over and over again in order to embrace all the possibilities.

It is perhaps all the more fortunate for Christians that it is difficult to give only one

definition of *epiousios* (daily? supernatural? future-eschatological? eucharistic?). We need all that "daily bread" can mean, and we must depend upon God for it.

We also yearn for a life of complete fulfillment in the kingdom of heaven, which is often described as a feast (see Isa 25:6-9)—and what is a feast without bread? And by our very baptismal nature, there is only one bread that can nurture eternal life within us: the bread of the Eucharist (see John 6:53-58).

And forgive us our debts, as we forgive our debtors. In praying about debt, is Jesus concerned about financial matters? Are we to pray for debt relief? Biblical scholars assure us that "debt" in this context was another word for sin. This is clearly the case in Luke's version of the Lord's Prayer, where this verse is translated as "forgive us our sins / for we ourselves forgive everyone in debt to us" (11:4).

In his book *Sin: A History*, Gary Anderson traces the connection between debt and sin throughout both the Old and New Testaments. The link between debt and sin grew and developed over time, especially following the Babylonian exile (6th century BC). In Leviticus 25:4, God commands that farmland must enjoy a sabbath (lay fallow) every seventh year, but apparently this command was not observed. Second Chronicles interprets the devastating Babylonian exile as a debt Israel had to repay to the Lord for all the sabbatical years of rest they had failed to give farmland as required in Leviticus:

> Those who escaped the sword he [the king of the Chaldeans] carried captive to Babylon, where they became servants to him and his sons until the Persian kingdom came to power. All this was to fulfill the word of the LORD spoken by Jeremiah: Until the land has retrieved its lost sabbaths, during all the time it lies waste it shall have rest while seventy years are fulfilled. (2 Chr 36:20-21.)

Sin came to be understood as something more than just a violation of the moral code for which one needed forgiveness. Sin was understood as something that created a debt owed to God. Every sin placed the sinner in God's debt, owing something that had to be paid back in some way. Thus "debt" became a ready metaphor for sin. After the exile, debt became more than a metaphor; it led to an understanding that one could be released from the debt of sin (forgiven) through the practice of almsgiving.

In the Lord's Prayer we ask for forgiveness of our debts "as we forgive our debtors." The comparative "as" carries a great deal of meaning in this phrase. It could be understood as a causal link to our being forgiven. If so, the petition could be rephrased as "since we have forgiven our debtors, we now ask you to forgive our debts." Or it might offer us a real challenge: "Forgive our debts in the same way that we forgive our debtors." That should give us

pause! Of course, it is impossible for us to forgive as completely and thoroughly as God forgives. The prophet Isaiah assures us of this: "Come now, let us set things right, / says the LORD: / Though your sins be like scarlet, / they may become white as snow; / Though they be red like crimson, / they may become white as wool" (1:18). And also, "It is I, I, who wipe out, / for my own sake, your offenses; your sins I remember no more" (43:25).

God is depicted here as "forgetting" our sins, or wiping them out completely. It is difficult for us to forgive in the same way because we remember when others have hurt us, and that remembered pain renews our need to forgive. For guidance here, we might look to Matthew 18:21-22. There Peter famously asks Jesus how often he must forgive his brother. Seven times? he asks. No, Jesus tells him, *seventy-seven* times (where seven is a symbolic number

 The Lord's Prayer falls almost dead center in the Sermon on the Mount. It is the central prayer of all disciples of Jesus. Just as Jews pray the Shema Israel from memory as a hallmark of their identity and faith ("Hear O Israel!"; Deut 6:4-5), so Christians pray the Our Father from memory. Although this prayer exists in two versions, in Matthew and in Luke, the Matthean version is the one that the church has prayed for centuries, most likely under the influence of consistent liturgical usage. In fact, it is always prayed in the Mass just prior to the communion rite.
The chart below sets forth a comparison of the two versions. Scholars generally deem Luke's more streamlined version to be closer to the form that Jesus actually prayed. Matthew's version exhibits more liturgical influence.

Matthew's Version (6:9-13)	Luke's Version (11:2-4)
Our Father in heaven	Father
Hallowed be your name	Hallowed be your name
Your kingdom come	Your kingdom come
Your will be done on earth as in heaven	
Give us today our daily bread	Give us each day our daily bread
Forgive us our debts as we forgive our debtors	Forgive us our sins for we ourselves forgive everyone in debt to us
Do not subject us to the final test	Do not subject us to the final test
But deliver us from the evil one	

of fullness). We must forgive those who have sinned against us, but we must do it over and over again because we remember the hurt, and every time we remember, we must once again forgive. In the section that follows (18:23-35), Jesus tells the powerful parable of the Unforgiving Servant, which leaves no question as to the necessity of forgiving others as God has forgiven us.

While we cannot forgive as graciously and thoroughly as God forgives us, once we experience the joy of being forgiven by God, we dare not harden our hearts toward a fellow human who has sinned against us. The importance of this is stressed by Jesus, who reaffirms it just after teaching us how to pray: "If you forgive others their transgressions, your heavenly Father will forgive you. But if you do not forgive others, neither will your Father forgive your transgressions" (Matt 6:14-15).

And do not subject us to the final test. Most of us are used to asking "our Father" to "lead us not into temptation." In both Matthew and Luke, we find slightly different language: "do not subject us to the final test" (New American Bible, Revised Edition) or "do not bring us to the time of trial" (New Revised Standard Version). But the difference between our traditional, liturgical form and what we read in the Sermon on the Mount simply helps us explore the wider ramifications of a prayer we have become so familiar with that we may not always ponder our words carefully.

Trial, test, and temptation are three words often associated in Scripture with the human experience of confronting the prospect of doing something morally wrong in order to escape an ordeal of some sort. Throughout the New Testament, early Christians were given inspired advice in dealing with the widespread experience of having their faith tested:

No trial has come to you but what is human. God is faithful and will not let you be tried beyond your strength; but with the trial he will also provide a way out, so that you may be able to bear it. (1 Cor 10:13)

Beloved, do not be surprised that a trial by fire is occurring among you, as if something strange were happening to you. But rejoice to the extent that you share in the sufferings of Christ, so that when his glory is revealed you may also rejoice exultantly. (1 Pet 4:12-13)

Blessed is the man who perseveres in temptation, for when he has been proved he will receive the crown of life that he promised to those who love him. (Jas 1:12)

In the Beatitudes, Christ blessed those who are persecuted for the sake of righteousness (5:10) and told those who would be persecuted for his name's sake to rejoice (5:11-12). And in the verse at hand, in teaching his followers how to pray, Jesus reveals his concern for his followers' fragility in the severity of persecution that might arise.

Indeed, in Matthew and in all of our gospels, Jesus is explicit about knowing that a "final test" awaits even him:

"Behold, we are going up to Jerusalem, and the Son of Man will be handed over to the chief priests and the scribes, and they will condemn him to death, and hand him over to the Gentiles to be mocked and scourged and crucified, and he will be raised on the third day." (Matt 20:18-19)

Just before he is arrested, Jesus asks the Father if it is possible to be spared this final test: "My Father, if it is possible, let this cup pass from me; yet, not as I will, but as you will" (Matt 26:39).

Many contemporary Christians will never experience the kind of persecution or trial endured by Jesus or the early Christians (though we are mindful of those in our world who do suffer persecution for the sake of their faith). When we pray the Our Father, we most often think of temptation as the allure of sin. In this case, it is helpful to keep in mind that of course God would never "lead us" to that kind of tempting. As James writes, "No one experiencing temptation should say, 'I am being tempted by God'; for God is not subject to temptation to evil, and he himself tempts no one. Rather, each person is tempted when he is lured and enticed by his own desire" (1:13-14).

The ultimate temptation (or the "final test") is really any test—whether in the form of persecution demanding a denial of our faith, or any painful circumstance such as illness, accident, or tragedy—that would tax our faithfulness to the limit. Jesus teaches us to pray that such ordeals will never push us beyond our ability to endure them with our faith intact.

But deliver us from the evil one. Usually when we pray the Lord's Prayer, we ask to be delivered from "evil," not from "the evil one." The Greek of Matthew's text allows either translation, and it has been rendered both ways in highly respectable translations. Asking for deliverance from "the evil one" has become the preferred translation in the majority of modern English translations.

What about the doxology?

When we pray the Our Father at Mass, we pray a doxology, or a short praise (literally "glory saying") of God, at the end: "For the kingdom, the power and the glory are yours now and forever." Doxologies are a traditional Jewish way of ending prayer with praise of God (e.g., Ps 41:14). Although the doxology of the Our Father is not included in the earliest existing manuscripts of Matthew's gospel (indicating that it likely was not part of Jesus' original prayer), it is found in the Didache, a Christian "manual" of sorts that may have been written as early as the middle of the first century or as late as early second century AD. It is also found in later manuscripts of Matthew's gospel, indicating that the doxology was used with the Our Father in the first-century church.

Given that the devil is the one who tempts Jesus in the desert following his baptism (Matt 4:1-11), it is quite likely that Jesus is teaching his followers to pray for deliverance from the

> ### Teaching about Fasting
>
> [16]"When you fast, do not look gloomy like the hypocrites. They neglect their appearance, so that they may appear to others to be fasting. Amen, I say to you, they have received their reward. [17]But when you fast, anoint your head and wash your face, [18]so that you may not appear to others to be fasting, except to your Father who is hidden. And your Father who sees what is hidden will repay you.
>
> *continue*

devil. In the context of Matthew's version of the Lord's Prayer, the devil is the ultimate source of pressure experienced in the horrors of a final test ("do not subject us to the final test, but deliver us from the evil one"). While the devil is not named here, Jesus names the devil who tempts him in the desert as "Satan" (4:10). Since Jesus also names Peter as "Satan" when Peter refuses to accept that Jesus must suffer death in Jerusalem (16:21-23), we can understand Satan as the one who opposes the will of God. Thus in the last petition of the Lord's Prayer, we are asking to be delivered from Satan or any influence that would lead us astray from God's will.

Teaching about Fasting (6:16-18)

Fasting in its biblical context is abstaining from food for a day or longer. Fasting features prominently in the Bible as an important element of authentic worship and spirituality. Whether it is an individual fasting or the entire people of God, there can be more than one reason for observing a fast. In the Old Testament, we find examples of people fasting in order to seek divine guidance (Judg 20:26), to express repentance (Neh 9:1-2), to express sorrow at a time of grievous loss (1 Sam 31:12-13), or to accompany prayer (2 Sam 12:21-23).

After his baptism, Jesus enters the wilderness and fasts for forty days, at the end of which he is tempted by the devil. This most famous fast of all is often seen as Jesus' prayerful preparation for his ministry, which will culminate in his death and resurrection. Its duration of forty days is also seen as an indication, especially in Matthew, that Jesus regards his mission as the embodiment and culmination of salvation history, which began with God's deliverance of Israel from their slavery in Egypt. For Israel, called God's son in Hosea 11:1, salvation history began with a journey of forty years in the wilderness where the Israelites were faced with temptation. Where Israel failed, however, God's Son Jesus succeeds (Matt 4:1-11).

We read in the gospels that Jesus' disciples did not fast during the course of Jesus' ministry. Jesus likened their circumstance to being in the entourage of a bridegroom before his wedding, a time dedicated to feasting, not fasting (Matt 9:14-15). But Jesus, who began his ministry with fasting, clearly is not opposed to the practice. What can rob fasting of its efficacy as a tool of prayer, supplication, grief, or repentance, however, is a lack of proper motivation.

In Matthew 6:16-18, we are reminded once again not to put our pious acts on public display. Fasting is an activity that involves withdrawal from the most basic of human concerns—eating—in order to focus on God as our greatest need and highest priority in life. Jesus warns against fasting as a means of gaining credit as a spiritual person in the eyes of others, which can easily eclipse the true purpose of fasting as a way to seek God's will and presence in one's life.

Hearing Jesus' instructions to fast quietly and with clean faces can be very puzzling on Ash Wednesday, as we have our foreheads smeared with ashes at the beginning of a season for fasting. But our ashes are not a sign that we are fasting. They are not placed on our heads to show others that we are enduring a tough day of spiritual discipline. Instead, the ashes are another biblical sign of sorrow and repentance (as indicated by the words "Repent and believe in the Gospel"; see Dan 9:3-21; Jonah 3; Mark 1:15) and a reminder of our mortality ("Remember that you are dust, and to dust you shall return"; see Gen 2:7; 3:19; 18:27). Our repentance may be public, but our fast should be quiet and private, as Jesus teaches us here.

Treasure in Heaven (6:19-21)

The heavenly reward Jesus' disciples are to seek should not simply be equated with going to heaven when they die.

The Greek word for "treasure" can indicate either the place where valuables are kept (such as a treasure chest) or the valuables themselves. Here, Jesus is clearly speaking of the things we value most—what we treasure, not where we put those things. When we examine several of Jesus' parables about treasure—the parable of the treasure buried in a field and the parable of the pearl of great price (Matt 13:44-46)—the treasure and the pearl that are valued so highly are symbols of the kingdom of heaven:

> "The kingdom of heaven is like a treasure buried in a field, which a person finds and hides again, and out of joy goes and sells all that he has and buys that field." (Matt 13:44)

> "[T]he kingdom of heaven is like a merchant searching for fine pearls. When he finds a pearl of great price, he goes and sells all that he has and buys it." (Matt 13:45-46)

In these verses of the Sermon on the Mount, Jesus is summarizing his warnings about performing righteous deeds for the benefit of public recognition and focusing his disciples' attention on the singular importance of the kingdom of heaven. Storing up treasure in heaven means to seek a heavenly reward rather than an earthly one. The realm where God's will is done is surely heaven, but putting our treasure there means seeking and performing God's will on earth, so that ultimately the kingdom of heaven will not just be in that "far off realm" called heaven but also here on earth. After all, in the Lord's Prayer, disciples are taught to pray: "Your kingdom come, your will be done, on earth as in heaven" (Matt 6:10).

Jesus always holds out an offer to those willing to pay the price by listening to and acting upon his words: the gift of entry into the kingdom of heaven. As he proclaimed at the very beginning of his ministry: "Repent, for the kingdom of heaven is at hand" (Matt 4:17). That initial entry may only be a first few steps into a vast and infinite kingdom, but its availability in the present to those who are willing to pay the price should never be doubted.

Lesson Three

EXPLORING LESSON THREE

1. Witnessing a heroic or charitable act can be inspiring, giving us hope for humanity and possibly prompting more good deeds from others (see 5:16). Why then would Jesus criticize performing righteous deeds in public (6:1-5)?

   It depends on the reason someone is doing the act — is it for their praise or for God's?

2. What differences (in content, in your emotions, or in your spirit) do you find between your private prayer and the prayer you engage in publicly, such as liturgical or communal prayer (6:5-8)?

   In my private prayer, it feels more like an intimate time between myself & God. Communal prayer feels more rote.

3. What emotions or internal responses do you experience in addressing God as "Father" (6:9)? How do you most often address God in your prayers?

   Lord or God or Father.

4. When we pray "your kingdom come" (6:10), what are we asking for?

   For the kingdom to come on earth.

5. What is meant by "our daily bread" (6:11)? Why is its meaning somewhat uncertain?

_____

_____

_____

_____

_____

6. How is our own spiritual welfare connected to forgiving others who have wronged us (6:12, 14-15)? (See 18:21-35.)

_____

_____

_____

_____

_____

7. Most of us have learned to pray the Our Father with the phrase "lead us not into temptation." How does the phrase Jesus uses in Matthew 6:13 ("do not subject us to the final test") add meaning to that request?

_____

_____

_____

_____

_____

8. a) Why has fasting been a traditional Jewish and Christian practice (6:16-18)? What is its purpose?

_____

_____

_____

b) What have been your own experiences of fasting? Have you found fasting to be a beneficial practice in your own spiritual life?

_____

_____

_____

9. Identify some of the ways you try to make your time, talent, and treasure an investment in the kingdom of heaven (6:19-21).

Almsgiving — time, talent, treasure

Trying to be more minamalistic

Sharing from excess

CLOSING PRAYER

Prayer

"For where your treasure is, there also will your heart be." (Matt 6:21)

Help us, Lord, to discover our treasure in you. As we examine our investments of energy, money, and time, give us the ability to put aside whatever keeps us from participating in your kingdom. We pray this day in thanksgiving for all that helps us maintain perspective, especially . . .

LESSON FOUR

Matthew 6:22–7:29

Begin your personal study and group discussion with a simple and sincere prayer such as:

Prayer

Jesus, you teach us to listen to your words and imitate your deeds. Be with me now as I listen for your voice, and help me to become more like you.

Read the Bible text of Matthew 6:22–7:29 found in the outside columns of pages 62–72, highlighting what stands out to you.

Read the accompanying commentary to add to your understanding.

Respond to the questions on pages 73–75, Exploring Lesson Four.

The Closing Prayer on page 75 is for your personal use and may be used at the end of group discussion.

> ### The Light of the Body
>
> [22]"The lamp of the body is the eye. If your eye is sound, your whole body will be filled with light; [23]but if your eye is bad, your whole body will be in darkness. And if the light in you is darkness, how great will the darkness be.
>
> ### God and Money
>
> [24]"No one can serve two masters. He will either hate one and love the other, or be devoted to one and despise the other. You cannot serve God and mammon.
>
> *continue*

6:22–7:29 DEPENDENCE UPON GOD

The Light of the Body (6:22-23)

The eye and the entire neural network that makes seeing possible are both complex and magnificent. Today we know far more about how vision occurs—how we can see what we see—than was known in the first century. At that time it was simply taken for granted that the eye itself generated the internal light that made vision possible. It seemed obvious that "seeing" was something that happened inside one's self.

Today we know the light that enables our physical vision comes from the sun or other light sources and enters our eyes from outside. But of course Jesus is using the language and understanding of his time. He isn't teaching science but a spiritual truth concerning the kind of spiritual enlightenment that leads to righteousness. It is, after all, not the eye that determines the way we look at the world, but what we choose to set our eyes upon and the moral framework within us that evaluates what we see.

If the light that fills us is goodness, we will be good and just people. If instead we are filled with the darkness of moral corruption, "how great will the darkness be"!

Every one of us was born with a light-emitting flame or spark within us. Everyone has been created in the image of God. Catholics have never accepted that it is possible to be human and not to bear within us some trace of that divine image. How do we fan the light-producing flame within each of us? Paul gives us some excellent advice:

> Finally, brothers, whatever is true, whatever is honorable, whatever is just, whatever is pure, whatever is lovely, whatever is gracious, if there is any excellence and if there is anything worthy of praise, think about these things. (Phil 4:8)

God and Money (6:24)

The Aramaic term "mammon" was not used in the Old Testament, but by Jesus' day, it had become an idiomatic reference not just to money but to those material possessions that were deemed most valuable. Jesus offers a keen insight that what is most desired in life is one's ultimate master. Desire controls the heart, and the heart is the prisoner of what one desires. An entire religion has grown up around this insight: Buddhism. Unlike Buddhism, Christianity does not reject desire. Instead, Jesus seeks to *refocus* our desire.

We have looked at the parable of the pearl of great price, where mammon in the form of a precious pearl is the focus of a merchant's desire to the point that he is willing to pay all that he has to obtain it. Jesus understands desire for mammon, but when he speaks of mammon as a slave master or as an object of supreme value, his goal is to create a desire for something far more valuable than mammon: the kingdom of heaven.

Unfortunately, the mention of "masters" may dampen our desire! Who wants to have any master at all? Isn't it better to be free? To desire God—which makes God one's master— is to accept the reign of God. The reign of God, which Matthew usually refers to as the king- dom of heaven, is the "pearl of great price." To desire God is to desire the source of all life, all goodness, all that could possibly be called treasure.

Here Jesus is also issuing a grave warning. At some point in our lives we may have em- barked on a journey to find the most valuable pearl of all and may have even been gifted with the revelation that the pearl we seek is the kingdom of heaven. But if our vision falls short and we become distracted by baubles, the baubles will become our master, and the God of all goodness will no longer hold the reins in our lives.

Dependence on God (6:25-34)

Many of us know what it is like to live from paycheck to paycheck, with nothing left over for those inevitable rainy days. It may seem that Jesus is glossing over actual need when he says, "do not worry about your life, what you will eat . . ." (6:25). But the testimony of the gospel is that Jesus is aware of the prevalence of hunger and thirst. Twice in Matthew's gos- pel (14:13-21; 15:32-39), Jesus feeds those who grow hungry. In Matthew 25, he assures his disciples that those who feed the hungry are actually feeding him, and that they will be given an eternal reward:

> "Come, you who are blessed by my Father. Inherit the kingdom prepared for you from the foundation of the world. For I was hungry and you gave me food, I was thirsty and you

> ### Dependence on God
>
> [25]"Therefore I tell you, do not worry about your life, what you will eat [or drink], or about your body, what you will wear. Is not life more than food and the body more than clothing? [26]Look at the birds in the sky; they do not sow or reap, they gather nothing into barns, yet your heavenly Father feeds them. Are not you more important than they? [27]Can any of you by worrying add a single moment to your life-span? [28]Why are you anxious about clothes? Learn from the way the wild flowers grow. They do not work or spin. [29]But I tell you that not even Solomon in all his splendor was clothed like one of them. [30]If God so clothes the grass of the field, which grows today and is thrown into the oven tomorrow, will he not much more provide for you, O you of little faith? [31]So do not worry and say, 'What are we to eat?' or 'What are we to drink?' or 'What are we to wear?' [32]All these things the pagans seek. Your heavenly Father knows that you need them all. [33]But seek first the kingdom [of God] and his righteousness, and all these things will be given you besides. [34]Do not worry about tomorrow; tomorrow will take care of itself. Sufficient for a day is its own evil.
>
> *continue*

gave me drink, a stranger and you welcomed me, naked and you clothed me, ill and you cared for me, in prison and you visited me." (25:34-36)

In the Sermon on the Mount, Jesus is not telling the crowds or his disciples that they will have every need met by simply believing and trusting in God's benevolence. Instead, he is urging them to make the kingdom of heaven their purpose in life, and then their basic needs will be met (6:33).

But what does it mean to make the king- dom of heaven our top priority? And how does this lead to the fulfillment of our needs?

In the last century, psychologist Abraham Maslow encapsulated in a simple scale how humans determine what is important in life. Maslow's hierarchy of human needs is most commonly depicted as a pyramid of ascending needs. According to Maslow, one must satisfy the needs one level at a time, beginning at the bottom of the pyramid.

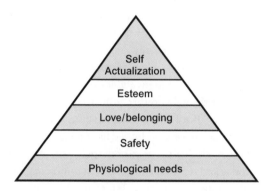

In the Sermon on the Mount, Jesus' teachings address several matters pertinent to Maslow's hierarchy. Among the *physiological needs*, food and clothing are very important. When Jesus asks if life is not more than these, he is asking a rhetorical question. Those who heard him may well have experienced real hunger in their lives, but they still wanted their lives to be about something more. Imagine struggling with issues as basic as food, clothing, and shelter, and then hearing that God offers a life far more enriching than the fight for survival.

Jesus urges a leap of faith for those who have received their most basic needs today but are worried about what they will eat or wear tomorrow: set your sight on the kingdom of heaven, and all these other things will fall into place.

Tradition tells us that Jesus was a woodworker, a carpenter. We really do not know how long he labored with his hands to make a living. We do know that at least by the time of John's arrest and imprisonment, he had dedicated his life to proclaiming the Good News that the kingdom of heaven was at hand (Matt 4:12-17). Shortly thereafter, he called the brothers Peter and Andrew and the brothers John

and James to abandon their livelihoods at fishing to come and follow him (4:18-22). They were to leave behind their homes (their shelter) and the daily labors that clothed and fed them.

Shortly after the conclusion of the Sermon on the Mount, Jesus has a warning for a scribe who wants to become a follower:

> A scribe approached and said to him, "Teacher, I will follow you wherever you go." Jesus answered him, "Foxes have dens and birds of the sky have nests, but the Son of Man has nowhere to rest his head." (8:19-20)

How do Jesus and his disciples survive? For the most part, they depend on support from other followers, chiefly (and maybe surprisingly) the women who accompany them (Matt 27:55; Mark 15:40-41; especially Luke 8:1-3). This tells us that Jesus is encouraging his followers to depend on God, but he is not saying that God's care for them will come without human care, concern, or labor. While Jesus does ask some of his followers to give up their livelihoods and possessions, clearly others are wealthy enough to accompany him on the way and to pay what is necessary to meet the group's physical needs.

Beyond the physiological, according to Maslow, is our *need for safety*. Without some assurance of safety, we would be living with fear that would easily prevent us from attending to anything but basic security. But as we see in the gospel, Jesus even addresses the concern for safety in a counterintuitive way. He deliberately sets himself on a path that will lead to death, and he encourages his followers to do the same. They are not to concern themselves with safety:

> Then Jesus said to his disciples, "Whoever wishes to come after me must deny himself, take up his cross, and follow me. For whoever wishes to save his life will lose it, but whoever loses his life for my sake will find it." (16:24-25)

Neither are his followers to be afraid of those who might mean to harm them:

"[D]o not be afraid of those who kill the body but cannot kill the soul; rather, be afraid of the one who can destroy both soul and body in Gehenna." (10:28)

Once again Jesus is aware of our needs as humans, but he continues to call us to look beyond even our most basic needs, and to do so by responding to something of even greater significance.

Jesus' call to his disciples in Matthew 6:25-34 (and to any in the crowd who would dare to think of themselves as eventual followers) becomes even more interesting as we move up Maslow's hierarchy to the *need for a sense of belonging*. It is said that this need is so great that it is responsible for both our most altruistic and most vile behaviors. Martyrs die for their community of faith, soldiers die for their country, and parents die to protect their children. On the other hand, suicide bombers blow themselves and others apart believing it is for the good of their religious community, political powers engage in genocide in order to protect the "purity" of their own ethnic groups, and children will enter gangs and engage in deadly violence to obtain a sense of belonging.

In Matthew (and elsewhere), Jesus challenges even our most basic sense of belonging to our families:

"I have come to set
a man 'against his father,
a daughter against her mother,
and a daughter against her mother-in-law;
and one's enemies will be those of his
household.'

"Whoever loves father or mother more than me is not worthy of me, and whoever loves son or daughter more than me is not worthy of me." (10:35-37)

Jesus challenges familial belonging by offering what could be an even stronger sense of belonging: association with Jesus and his kingdom (see also Mark 10:28-30).

In Matthew 23:8, Jesus tells his disciples that they are all brothers. Once this "band of brothers" spreads his Gospel throughout the Roman Empire (with help from the apostle Paul and others), all who accept their message and are baptized will also be regarded as brothers and sisters in Christ.

According to Maslow, once we have gained a sense of belonging, we need or yearn for the *respect and esteem of others*. For Maslow, esteem goes beyond the respect we might enjoy within our families or among our most intimate friends. The need for esteem may extend into a desire for fame—to be highly regarded because one has made a positive impact on a large number of people. Respect from others may even be

Jesus tells us not to worry, but **worry and stress** are so common in our daily lives. How do we stop worrying? Here are some ideas based on Jesus' words in 6:25-34:

- We can look beyond our current situation to see the "bigger picture" of God's care for us, now and into eternity (6:25).

- We can keep our expectations simple, like birds and flowers. We don't need to have the best or be the best. We simply need God's loving care (6:26-30).

- We can remember how much God values each one of us (6:26).

- We can remind ourselves that worrying is futile. It doesn't solve our problems or lengthen our lives (6:27, 34).

- We can prioritize our lives in a way that reflects our love for God and our brothers and sisters. God already knows what we need, so we can spend less time worrying and more time being the love of Christ in the world (6:31-33).

spoken of as admiration. Earlier in the Sermon on the Mount, Jesus clearly criticized the pursuit of public admiration, but he did so in a way that also acknowledged its importance to individuals in his society:

> "When you give alms, do not blow a trumpet before you, as the hypocrites do in the synagogues and in the streets to win the praise of others. Amen, I say to you, they have received their reward." (6:2)

> When you pray, do not be like the hypocrites, who love to stand and pray in the synagogues and on street corners so that others may see them. Amen, I say to you, they have received their reward." (6:5)

Public esteem is a reward, but pursuing esteem is the wrong reason for charity or prayer. Again, Jesus is teaching his disciples to forego a basic need (the desire for praise and admiration) in order to pursue something more important (a pure focus on God), which is counterintuitive to Maslow's approach to human needs.

The crowning need on Maslow's hierarchical pyramid is *self-actualization*. When seeking to be all that we are capable of being, we are committing ourselves to realizing—or "actualizing"—our potential. As an example, for years the US Army used the slogan "Be all you can be" in its endeavors to fill its ranks with committed volunteers.

Unfortunately, the idea of self-actualization has actually emboldened many to abandon commitments and obligations to their spouses, children, and others in the endeavor to find themselves. When "finding ourselves" becomes our highest goal in life, it sometimes results in seeing others as impediments to our personal fulfillment, even the very ones who have sacrificed the most to give us a sense of belonging.

It is safe to say that the phrase "self-actualization" never fell from the lips of Jesus. The closest Jesus ever came to addressing the notion of achieving one's highest purpose might be found in this paradoxical teaching in Matthew 10:39: "Whoever finds his life will lose it, and whoever loses his life for my sake will find it." If true self-actualization entails embracing a divine calling to achieve a life-giving purpose, even a willingness to forfeit any other good or personal need, then the Sermon on the Mount can indeed be understood as a call to self-actualization.

Interestingly, Maslow came to understand that the quest for meaning in life can arise precisely because of an experience of loss, or a threat to any or all of the needs that lie below self-actualization on his hierarchy. Awareness of unmet needs can lead someone to dedicate his or her life to addressing the needs of those who are suffering. Christ himself modeled this heroic suffering.

We can certainly acknowledge the common sense behind Maslow's hierarchy of needs. We are not likely to ask those who are hungry or cold about their highest purpose in life. And indeed, our Christian obligation toward them is well stated in James 2:15-16:

> If a brother or sister has nothing to wear and has no food for the day, and one of you says to them, "Go in peace, keep warm, and eat well," but you do not give them the necessities of the body, what good is it?

And yet, as Christians we can never allow our own hunger or physical needs to nullify our highest calling. We are to trust that our heavenly Father knows our every need. We are to seek first the kingdom of heaven and let tomorrow "take care of itself" (6:31-34).

Judging Others (7:1-5)

That Jesus' teaching against judging others was at the core of his message is demonstrated by its presence outside the gospels, elsewhere in the New Testament. Around the same time the Gospel of Matthew was written (ca. AD 85), the Letter of James was challenging believers with the same message:

> Do not speak evil of one another, brothers. Whoever speaks evil of a brother or judges his brother speaks evil of the law and judges the

law. If you judge the law, you are not a doer of the law but a judge. There is one lawgiver and judge who is able to save or to destroy. Who then are you to judge your neighbor? (Jas 4:11-12)

Around thirty years earlier, Paul offered his own warning about judging others in his Letter to the Romans: "Therefore, you are without excuse, every one of you who passes judgment. For by the standard by which you judge another you condemn yourself, since you, the judge, do the very same things" (2:1).

One synonym for judgment is discernment. Discernment is essential for a Christian. Discernment is the ability to aid one's conscience by applying knowledge from a good set of moral principles to any given situation or activity before entering that situation or engaging in the activity. Discernment may tell you that something that someone else is doing is wrong, but making that discernment is not the same as judging the person.

In the religious milieu of Jesus' time and place, judging others meant placing them in one of two categories: people were either righteous or sinners. A righteous person was one who followed the law and was "in good standing" with God. A sinner, on the other hand, was a moral reprobate already living under God's judgment.

In Jesus' time there was a religious sect within Judaism, the Essenes, who regarded all other Jews as sinners who, on the looming Day of Judgment, would be utterly destroyed. The gospels depict the Pharisees as another sect within Judaism that made sharp distinctions between the righteous and sinners. Their hostility toward Jesus is frequently rooted in Jesus' suspicious behavior of freely associating with sinners, even to the extent of eating with them.

In Matthew 9:10-11, we are told that it was the Pharisees who noted that Jesus ate with Matthew the tax collector and his friends and who found Jesus' behavior questionable:

While he was at table in his [Matthew's] house, many tax collectors and sinners came and sat with Jesus and his disciples. The Pharisees saw

CHAPTER 7

Judging Others

[1]"Stop judging, that you may not be judged. [2]For as you judge, so will you be judged, and the measure with which you measure will be measured out to you. [3]Why do you notice the splinter in your brother's eye, but do not perceive the wooden beam in your own eye? [4]How can you say to your brother, 'Let me remove that splinter from your eye,' while the wooden beam is in your eye? [5]You hypocrite, remove the wooden beam from your eye first; then you will see clearly to remove the splinter from your brother's eye.

continue

this and said to his disciples, "Why does your teacher eat with tax collectors and sinners?"

Eating with sinners was deemed by the Pharisees to be sinful on two levels. First, it implied guilt by association: why would anyone eat with sinners unless he also was a sinner? Second, it was assumed that sinners would pay little attention to the rules of religious purity and would therefore likely be unclean, which at least threatened those who associated with them with uncleanliness. A righteous person would be protective of his or her ability to engage in religious activities requiring ritual purity. Jesus' lack of concern in this area did not reflect well on his "righteousness"!

Eating with sinners was central to Jesus' mission "to the lost sheep of the house of Israel" (Matt 10:6, 15:24). Jesus had something to offer sinners: love, acceptance, and forgiveness. He had nothing to offer those who already counted themselves among the righteous. When the Pharisees questioned Jesus' disciples as to why he ate with sinners, Jesus heard their question and responded: "Those who are well do not need a physician, but the sick do" (Matt 9:12).

Passing judgment, in the cultural milieu of Jesus' time, created a deep division in society

---

Pearls before Swine

⁶"Do not give what is holy to dogs, or throw your pearls before swine, lest they trample them underfoot, and turn and tear you to pieces.

The Answer to Prayers

⁷"Ask and it will be given to you; seek and you will find; knock and the door will be opened to you. ⁸For everyone who asks, receives; and the one who seeks, finds; and to the one who knocks, the door will be opened. ⁹Which one of you

continue

---

and assumed that the vast majority of people were living outside the blessings of Israel's covenant relationship with God. Jesus turned this view on its head by warning that it is actually the ones who pass judgment who are most in danger of stepping outside their covenant relationship with God. That covenant was embodied in "the law" that Jesus came to fulfill (Matt 5:17), and one of the ways he fulfilled it was to extend God's love to those whom the "righteous" condemned as "sinners."

Pearls before Swine (7:6)

Both dogs and swine were considered to be unclean animals by first-century Jews. Observant Jews would never allow dogs to live inside their personal dwellings, and swine—while a prized food source in much of the Mediterranean region—were forbidden as food (Lev 11:4-8). Here, Jesus uses these animals as contemptuous terms in reference to Gentiles. Later in the gospel, he will implicitly refer to the Canaanite woman seeking healing for her daughter as a dog: "It is not right to take the food of the children and throw it to the dogs" (15:26). We might note, however, that she is successful in arguing with Jesus that even dogs get fed scraps, and in healing her daughter, it is no scrap that Jesus offers her!

As uncomfortable as modern readers may be with Jesus using this type of language, in Matthew's gospel, Jesus is consistent in limiting his ministry to his own people, and he tells his disciples that they, too, are to focus their evangelizing endeavors on their own people and no one else:

> Jesus sent out these twelve after instructing them thus, "Do not go into pagan territory or enter a Samaritan town. Go rather to the lost sheep of the house of Israel. As you go, make this proclamation: 'The kingdom of heaven is at hand.'" (Matt 10:5-7)

After the resurrection, Matthew's community will be made aware that the Gospel is to be announced to all the nations. The risen Jesus instructs his followers:

> "Go, therefore, and make disciples of all nations, baptizing them in the name of the Father, and of the Son, and of the holy Spirit, teaching them to observe all that I have commanded you." (Matt 28:19-20a)

There is a timeless message within Jesus' warning about tossing pearls to swine. Beyond its ethnic overtones, this saying of Jesus tells us that there are people who only have contempt for any message associated with the Gospel. If the Christian message is only going to be met with mockery, or perhaps even violence, then it is better to save it for those who have some hunger for the truth.

The Answer to Prayers (7:7-11)

Jesus tells us to ask, to seek, and to knock. What is not directly stated in this passage is *what* we are to ask for, *what* we are to seek, or on *what door* we should be knocking. The Greek word for "ask" really means "desire." The child Jesus uses as an example asks for a fish, and it may be assumed that a child who asks for a fish is hungry. He or she desires to eat. If we, who are imperfect and sinful, give good things to our children when they desire them, then surely God will give good things to us if we desire them. Perhaps the lesson here includes examining what we ask for and whether or not it reflects a desire for what is truly good.

The Letter of James makes this point very clearly: "You ask but do not receive, because you ask wrongly, to spend it on your passions" (Jas 4:3).

In Luke's version of this saying, Jesus has one very specific good in mind when he assures his disciples that if they ask they will receive: "If you then, who are wicked, know how to give good gifts to your children, how much more will the Father in heaven give the holy Spirit to those who ask him?" (Luke 11:13).

In Matthew's account Jesus is not this specific, but like the child who is hungry for a fish, if we ask for good gifts, we will receive them. When we place this teaching within the entire context of the Sermon on the Mount, it is as disciples intent on seeking the kingdom of heaven that we ask for anything in prayer. Whether asking, seeking, or knocking, a disciple of Jesus is someone who is entirely dependent upon God for receiving whatever gifts are needed to fulfill God's will.

The *Catechism of the Catholic Church* identifies five basic forms of prayer: blessing, petition, intercession, thanksgiving, and praise (*CCC* 2644). Interestingly, Jesus' teachings primarily focus on **petitionary prayer**—asking for the things we want or need. This may seem to be a "lowly" type of prayer, but Jesus teaches that it is pleasing to God. Petitionary prayer humbly acknowledges our total reliance on God and our trust in God to take care of us. Jesus encourages perseverance in our petitions (Luke 11:5-13; 18:1-8), and he promises his disciples: "[W]hatever you ask in my name, I will do, so that the Father may be glorified in the Son. If you ask anything in my name, I will do it" (John 14:13-14).

The Golden Rule (7:12)

Scholars of comparative religions claim, with abundant evidence, that every major reli-

would hand his son a stone when he asks for a loaf of bread, ¹⁰or a snake when he asks for a fish? ¹¹If you then, who are wicked, know how to give good gifts to your children, how much more will your heavenly Father give good things to those who ask him.

The Golden Rule

¹²"Do to others whatever you would have them do to you. This is the law and the prophets.

continue

gion of the world teaches some version of what has come down to us from Jesus as "the golden rule."

At around the same time as Jesus, Hillel, one of the most highly respected Pharisees and rabbis of all time, taught what we now call the golden rule. While Jesus phrased it in positive terms ("Do to others whatever you would have them do to you"), Hillel expressed the same sentiment in negative terms: "What you hate, don't do to others." Hillel also claimed that this maxim summed up the entire Torah.

The equation of the golden rule with the entirety of the law and the prophets (that is, of the entire Old Testament) has the effect of humanizing all the commandments and precepts of the Scriptures as Jesus knew them. In a similar way, later in Matthew's account Jesus will summarize the law with the commands to love God and neighbor (22:34-40). Both the golden rule and the love commands demonstrate the priority Jesus gives to relationships as the context for obedience to the law.

As universal as the golden rule is, when pronounced by Jesus in the context of the Sermon on the Mount, it becomes a touchstone that brings to heart and mind all that Jesus teaches there. Because it is stated as a positive command ("do to others") rather than a negative command ("don't do to others"), the golden rule implies an active stance toward all others. Because Jesus teaches love of enemies

> ### The Narrow Gate
>
> ¹³"Enter through the narrow gate; for the gate is wide and the road broad that leads to destruction, and those who enter through it are many. ¹⁴How narrow the gate and constricted the road that leads to life. And those who find it are few.
>
> ### False Prophets
>
> ¹⁵"Beware of false prophets, who come to you in sheep's clothing, but underneath are ravenous wolves. ¹⁶By their fruits you will know them. Do people pick grapes from thornbushes, or figs from thistles? ¹⁷Just so, every good tree bears good fruit, and a rotten tree bears bad fruit. ¹⁸A good tree cannot bear bad fruit, nor can a rotten tree bear good fruit. ¹⁹Every tree that does not bear good fruit will be cut down and thrown into the fire. ²⁰So by their fruits you will know them.
>
> *continue*

in the sermon (Matt 5:44), those who are followers of Jesus cannot simply resist doing evil to their enemies. They must deal with them in the manner in which they would most hope their enemies would treat them, that is, with love and compassion.

The Narrow Gate (7:13-14)

The Sermon on the Mount turns toward its conclusion by noting that there are two contrasting ways to live, one of which leads to life and the other to destruction. Jesus' implied warning about the broad road that leads to destruction is addressed to those who are already his disciples or who have at least traveled a distance to hear his wisdom. They are looking for guidance. Jesus uses a gated passageway as a metaphor for the life we live as his followers. Not only is it necessary to choose the right path, but that path begins on the other side of a very narrow gate.

In the time and place of Jesus' ministry, gates marked the entrances to almost everything. Cities had gates, properties had gates,

roads and paths had gates. Just like today, gates existed for security purposes in order to control the right of passage into places of importance.

Jesus is clear that we will not accidently find ourselves upon the path that leads to life. Rather, we have to consciously choose it, to deliberately set out on it from a beginning point: at the gate that is narrow, that opens up to an arduous and narrow path.

This teaching asserts that we cannot be on the path that leads to life unless we are aware of it. Being on the path to life demands intentionality, a consciousness that we have passed through a gate with decisiveness and that the steps we are taking on the path are taking us in the right direction.

False Prophets (7:15-20)

Scripture scholars tell us that it is best to read these verses in the context of Matthew's church in the decades after the death and resurrection of Jesus. This does not mean that this teaching wasn't in conformity with what Jesus himself taught, but that the warning was seen as especially important to Matthew's writing of the Sermon on the Mount at a time when his community was being disturbed by preachers and teachers—"prophets"—who did not share Matthew's concern for the well-being of the community.

In biblical times, the role of prophets was to inform God's people, especially those who were responsible for the welfare of God's people (such as royalty and ministerial leaders, both of whom were often referred to as shepherds), of how God was calling the people to live in the present. In biblical times, the role of prophets was to inform God's people and, in a special way, the leaders of God's people, that they had a responsibility to communicate God's will and to respond to God's call. God's prophets reminded the community of their identity as covenant people and reminded their leaders to encourage the growth of good fruit in daily life in the community. True prophets recognize that the fruit of tomorrow is planted in the seeds of today, and that the judgment of tomorrow lies in the behavior choices of today.

We still need prophets to awaken us to our collective calling as disciples in our own time and place. The danger of false prophets still exists, and Jesus' warning concerning them tells us how to recognize them: no matter how they appear (clothed like meek, gentle sheep), they are at heart "ravenous wolves." Wolves devour sheep. False prophets only seek their own welfare, their own glory. They are intent on gaining a following for themselves, often by taking sheep away from the rest of the flock. Unity has always been a hallmark of discipleship.

On the other hand, Jesus also tells us how to recognize true prophets: their lives will produce good fruit. These "good trees" have a nourishing, fruitful role in our church communities, just as they did in the time of Matthew. Jesus' warning encourages us to listen to the voices that unite and bear fruit, and to recognize as "false" those voices that divide and devour.

The True Disciple (7:21-23)

In this passage the kingdom of heaven is spoken of as a thing, or event, to take place at a future time. It is no longer, as it has been frequently expressed by Jesus, a reality opening up in the present in some mysterious way as a result of Jesus' presence, in his deeds and through his teaching (see especially Matt 4:17). Theologians speak of the "dual nature" of the kingdom of heaven (or the kingdom of God) as something that both *is* and *is yet to come*.

The frightening aspect of this particular teaching is that it is possible to do great deeds in the name of Jesus—even deeds of healing!—and still be sent away by Jesus when he finally establishes the kingdom once and for all. Some who claim to know Jesus will be told that Jesus never knew *them*.

Those who will enter the kingdom of heaven are those who do the will of the Father. The whole of the Sermon on the Mount has been an explication of what it means to do the will of the Father. It means to become a disciple of Jesus and to observe all that he teaches—to be changed, to become perfect, to bear good

The True Disciple

²¹"Not everyone who says to me, 'Lord, Lord,' will enter the kingdom of heaven, but only the one who does the will of my Father in heaven. ²²Many will say to me on that day, 'Lord, Lord, did we not prophesy in your name? Did we not drive out demons in your name? Did we not do mighty deeds in your name?' ²³Then I will declare to them solemnly, 'I never knew you. Depart from me, you evildoers.'

The Two Foundations

²⁴"Everyone who listens to these words of mine and acts on them will be like a wise man who built his house on rock. ²⁵The rain fell, the floods came, and the winds blew and buffeted the house. But

continue

fruit. Later, in Matthew 25, Jesus will explain what this kind of life looks like. These are the people he will welcome into his kingdom:

> "'Come, you who are blessed by my Father. Inherit the kingdom prepared for you from the foundation of the world. For I was hungry and you gave me food, I was thirsty and you gave me drink, a stranger and you welcomed me, naked and you clothed me, ill and you cared for me, in prison and you visited me.' Then the righteous will answer him and say, 'Lord, when did we see you hungry and feed you, or thirsty and give you drink? When did we see you a stranger and welcome you, or naked and clothe you? When did we see you ill or in prison, and visit you?' And the king will say to them in reply, 'Amen, I say to you, whatever you did for one of these least brothers of mine, you did for me.'" (Matt 25:34-40)

The Two Foundations (7:24-29)

Matthew concludes the Sermon on the Mount with Jesus' warning concerning the importance of taking to heart what he has taught it did not collapse; it had been set solidly on rock. ²⁶And everyone who listens to these words of mine but does not act on them will be like a fool who built his house on sand. ²⁷The rain fell, the floods came, and the winds blew and buffeted the house. And it collapsed and was completely ruined."

²⁸When Jesus finished these words, the crowds were astonished at his teaching, ²⁹for he taught them as one having authority, and not as their scribes.

in the sermon. Matthew wants his community (and all of his readers) to be more than listeners. They were, and we are, called to *act* on his words. Failure to do so will only end in disaster. Jesus, however, accentuates the positive by illustrating the benefit of hearing and acting on his word. The Sermon on the Mount lays the foundation for a life built upon the rock.

Matthew ends the Sermon on the Mount with what Scripture scholars call an *inclusio* (7:28-29). This means that Matthew has built a frame around the beginning and end of this most famous sermon in all of history by including key words from his introduction in the conclusion. Introducing the Sermon on the Mount, Matthew wrote of those who witnessed it, the crowds that had gathered around Jesus and the disciples: "When he saw the crowds, he went up the mountain, and after he had sat down, his disciples came to him" (5:1).

In his conclusion to the sermon, Matthew reminds us of the crowds and tells us of their astonishment at the authority with which Jesus taught. He doesn't mention the disciples in his conclusion, probably because the sermon has been primarily directed at the disciples. In Matthew, the crowds are fickle. Here on the mount, "the crowds" listen to Jesus with amazement. Later a "very large crowd" will hail him as "the Son of David" when he enters Jerusalem (21:8-9). But soon afterward, "the crowds" will shout, "Let him be crucified!" (27:21-23). But the disciples are also fickle. They who profess to be followers of Jesus (unlike the crowds) will all abandon him (26:56).

Matthew wants those who hear the Sermon on the Mount to think of themselves as disciples. More than *admiring* the words, we are to *act on them* as disciples. Knowing how hard it is to live up to Jesus' words, we need reminding that even disciples fail Jesus. They fail, but they come back to try again. Even if our dwellings have been swept off the sand by a flood, we can come back to the Sermon on the Mount to stand, barefoot and homeless if need be, upon the rock.

EXPLORING LESSON FOUR

1. In what ways do you experience the tension between serving God and serving mammon (6:24)? What concrete steps can you take to ensure you are serving God?

Obligations

Do them w/ a servant heart & quit fretting or feeling sorry for myself.

2. What things tend to worry you the most (6:25-34)? Are these worries connected to certain perceived needs in your life? How can you develop more trust in God's care? (See Phil 4:6-7.)

Long term health issues.

3. How does Maslow's hierarchy of needs help you reflect on Jesus' teachings on dependence on God (6:25-34)? How does what Jesus teaches in the Sermon on the Mount surpass Maslow's insights?

4. How can one avoid being judgmental without condoning immorality or poor choices (7:1-5)?

If speaking truth to immorality or poor choice try to put it into Gospel teachings. Have to remember we are all children of the Father & still love the "offenders".

Lesson Four

5. How do you protect the holy things in your life from those who would revile them (7:6)? At the same time, how do we share what we have been given in a way that attracts others to the Good News?

Hold them close to my heart — be thankful. Share my gifts given to me by God. Treat others as I want to be treated or Do What Jesus would do — and give Him the credit.

6. What good things do you think Jesus asks his disciples to ask for or seek (7:7-11)? (See Luke 11:9-13.)

Whatever we need to fulfill God's Will — Help in bringing the kingdom to fruition

7. What influence has the golden rule had on your life (7:12)?

Learned it as a youngster ✓ kept alive Thru out my life

8. We speak (and sing) of the wideness of God's mercy, and yet the gate and road to life is narrow and constricted (7:13-14). How can both be true?

Believe. if we live as disciples & keep trying the gate will be wide open. — So far to go yet.

9. What practices help to ensure that one is a true disciple known by Jesus (7:21-23) and that one's house is built on solid rock rather than shifting sand (7:24-27)?

Prayer — bible study — scripture.

10. What challenges you most in Jesus' teaching from the Sermon on the Mount?

Remembering that He is the giver — and I am receiver // giver to others.

CLOSING PRAYER

Prayer

[T]he crowds were astonished at his teaching,
for he taught them as one having authority
. . . (Matt 7:28-29)

Jesus, Master Teacher, transform us from listeners and spectators to disciples. Move us from wonder and awe to commitment and action. We desire your kingdom above all else, and we pray now for its coming: "Our Father, who art in heaven . . ."

75

SUGGESTED READING

Allison, Dale C. *The Sermon on the Mount: Inspiring the Moral Imagination.* New York: The Crossroad Publishing Co., 1999.

Carter, Warren. *What Are They Saying About Matthew's Sermon on the Mount?* New York: Paulist Press, 1994.

Crosby, Michael H., OFM Cap. *Spirituality of the Beatitudes: Matthew's Vision for the Church in an Unjust World.* New Revised Edition. Maryknoll, NY: Orbis Books, 2005.

Davies, W. D. *The Setting of the Sermon on the Mount.* New York: Cambridge University Press, 1977.

Lapide, Pinchas. Translated by Arlene Swidler. *The Sermon on the Mount: Utopia or Program for Action?* Maryknoll, NY: Orbis Books, 1986.

LaVerdiere, Eugene, SSS. *The Eucharist in the New Testament and the Early Church.* Collegeville, MN: Liturgical Press, 1996.

Matera, Frank. *The Sermon on the Mount: The Perfect Measure of the Christian Life.* Collegeville, MN: Liturgical Press, 2013.

Meier, John P. *The Vision of Matthew, Christ, Church, and Morality in the First Gospel.* Eugene, OR: Wipf & Stock Publishers, 2004.

Senior, Donald. *Matthew.* Abingdon New Testament Commentaries. Nashville: Abingdon Press, 1998.

Worth, Roland H., Jr. *The Sermon on the Mount: Its Old Testament Roots.* New York: Paulist Press, 1997.

PRAYING WITH YOUR GROUP

Because we know that the Bible allows us to hear God's voice, prayer provides the context for our study and sharing. By speaking and listening to God and each other, the discussion often grows to more deeply bond us to one another and to God.

At *the beginning and end of each lesson* simple prayers are provided for individual use, and also may be used within the group setting. Most of the closing prayers provided with each lesson relate directly to a theme from that lesson and encourage you to pray together for people and events in your local community.

Of course, there are many ways to center ourselves in God's presence as we gather together in groups around the word of God. We provide some additional suggestions here knowing you and your group will make prayer a priority as part of your gathering. These are simply alternative ways to pray if your group would like to try something different from those prayers provided in the previous pages.

Conversational Prayer

This form of prayer allows for the group members to pray in their own words in a way that is not intimidating. The group leader begins with Step One, inviting all to focus on the presence of Christ among them. After a few moments of quiet, the group leader invites anyone in the group to voice a prayer or two of thanksgiving; once that is complete, then anyone who has personal intentions may pray in their own words for their needs; finally, the group prays for the needs of others.

A suggested process:
In your own words, speak simple and short prayers to allow time for others to add their voices.

Focus on one "step" at a time, not worrying about praying for everything in your mental list at once.

Step One	Visualize Christ. Welcome him. Imagine him present with you in your group. Allow time for some silence.
Step Two	Gratitude opens our hearts. Use simple words such as, "Thank you, Lord, for . . ."
Step Three	Pray for your own needs knowing that others will pray with you. Be specific and honest. Use "I" and "me" language.

Step Four	Pray for others by name, with love.
	You may voice your agreement ("Yes, Lord").
	End with gratitude for sharing concerns.

Praying Like Ignatius

St. Ignatius Loyola, whose life and ministry are the foundation of the Jesuit community, invites us to enter into Scripture texts in order to experience the scenes, especially scenes of the gospels or other narrative parts of Scripture. Simply put, this is a method of creatively imagining the scene, viewing it from the inside, and asking God to meet you there. Most often, this is a personal form of prayer, but in a group setting, some of its elements can be helpful if you allow time for this process.

A suggested process:

- Select a scene from the chapters in the particular lesson.
- Read that scene out loud in the group, followed by some quiet time.
- Ask group members to place themselves in the scene (as a character, or as an onlooker) so that they can imagine the emotions, responses, and thinking that may have taken place. Notice the details and the tone, and imagine the interaction with the Lord that is taking place.
- Share with the group any insights that came to you in this quiet imagining.
- Allow each person in the group to thank God for some insight and to pray about some request that may have surfaced.

Sacred Reading (or Lectio Divina)

This method of prayer invites us to "listen with the ear of the heart" as St. Benedict's rule would say. We listen to the words and the phrasing, asking God to speak to our innermost being. Again, this method of prayer is most often used in an individual setting but may also be used in an adapted way within a group.

A suggested process:

- Select a scene from the chapters in the particular lesson.
- Read the scene out loud in the group, perhaps two times.
- Ask group members to ponder a word or phrase that stands out to them.
- The group members could then simply speak the word or phrase as a kind of litany of what was meaningful for your group.
- Allow time for more silence to ponder the words that were heard, asking God to reveal to you what message you are meant to hear, how God is speaking to you.
- Follow up with spoken intentions at the close of this group time.

REFLECTING ON SCRIPTURE

Reading Scripture is an opportunity not simply to learn new information but to listen to God who loves you. Pray that the same Holy Spirit who guided the formation of Scripture will inspire you to correctly understand what you read, and empower you to make what you read a part of your life.

The inspired word of God contains layers of meaning. As you make your way through passages of Scripture, whether studying a book of the Bible or focusing on a biblical theme, you may find it helpful to ask yourself these four questions:

What does the Scripture passage say?
Read the passage slowly and reflectively. Become familiar with it. If the passage you are reading is a narrative, carefully observe the characters and the plot. Use your imagination to picture the scene or enter into it.

What does the Scripture passage mean?
Read the footnotes in your Bible and the commentary provided to help you understand what the sacred writers intended and what God wants to communicate by means of their words.

What does the Scripture passage mean to me?
Meditate on the passage. God's word is living and powerful. What is God saying to you? How does the Scripture passage apply to your life today?

What am I going to do about it?
Try to discover how God may be challenging you in this passage. An encounter with God contains a challenge to know God's will and follow it more closely in daily life. Ask the Holy Spirit to inspire not only your mind but your life with this living word.